€18

Published by BookMan OÜ, Estonia

Copyright © Vello Vikerkaar 2009

Cover image by istockphoto.com

Cover and book design by Napo Monasterio

ISBN: 1-4392-5603-9

Many of the shorter stories in this book were originally published in the Estonian language in the weekly *Eesti Ekspress*, as well as the dailies, *Eesti Päevaleht* and *Postimees*. Some were later collected in the Estonian-language book, *Pikk jutt, sitt jutt: Kogutud lühijuttud*. "Meet Your Local Action Hero," in a slightly different form, was published in the American literary journal, *The Iconoclast*. Several of the stories were originally published in *The Huffington Post*.

INHERIT THE FAMILY
Marrying into
Eastern Europe

Stories by
Vello Vikerkaar

To Liina.
Who else?

Table of Contents

PART TWO: LONGER STUFF

WHAT THE HELL IS ESTONIA? the reader may be wondering, and knowing will come in handy when reading these stories. Estonia is a bit larger than Rhode Island and is located sixty miles south of Finland and an overnight boat ride east of Sweden. It's been occupied for most of its recorded history by just about everyone but the Polynesians (the Danes, Swedes, Germans, and Russians have run the place), though it was an independent nation between the two world wars and has been again since 1991. From 1948 to 1991 it was the westernmost point of the former Soviet Union, and some say the Russians wouldn't mind very much if they had it back. Despite their rather aggressive neighbor, Estonians are known as a quiet, nature-loving folk. They speak Estonian, a Finno-Ugric tongue related to Finnish and Hungarian, and most of the population speak another two or three languages, as well. That's enough to get you started, and if you at all paid attention to this paragraph, then you already know more than most people working at the US Department of State.

PART ONE: SHORT PIECES

❶ Inherit the Family

'**I**f this rabbit goes, I go, too." My wife's aunt had her hands locked to the cage, fingers twisted through the wires for a solid grip.

"Pack your bags then," I said. My hands were wrapped around the other side of the cage and I was pulling hard. "Give me the fucking rabbit!" I often switch to English when angry. While pulling for my half of the rabbit, I wondered why it was my job to fight with this 75-year-old woman who wouldn't permit me to give away the animal that had chewed through the electrical cords in the house? She wasn't even related to me.

There are all sorts of stories about Eastern Europe which circulated in Canada in the early 90s. One was that for a pair of Levi's blue jeans you could buy a car. It was said that for a pack of Marlboros you could have anything smaller. The women were purportedly both gorgeous and dangerous, capable of weaving especially wicked webs.

A few years after arriving in 1992, I married an Estonian woman. None of the warnings that circulated in Canada turned out to apply to Liina. What they should have warned me about were the standard marital issues which apply in every culture. Like the fact that when you marry the wife, you inherit the family.

In Estonia, when a relative gets old the young take care of her. In my North American culture, when a relative gets old we ship her off to the old folks' home. She usually goes willingly, because independence is such an ingrained part of our culture that she doesn't want to be a burden. We don't consider it cruel, though in some re-spects it surely is. I think the Estonian tradition is much more humane, a poetic role reversal where the young care for the old. It's beautiful. Or so I thought before I had first-hand experience.

I had met my wife's aunt on several occasions before we married, and I knew how important she'd been in Liina's life. The aunt had been the worldly role model. The old gal could be a real charmer, too, and liked to dress up and sashay through town, chatting up all the neighbors. I knew that when we built a house, we'd need to account for her. I imagined a sweet old woman who could help with the gardening, babysit the kids, and tell witty stories from a forgotten world. So we built a house in the garden district of Nõmme with a small apartment for her where she could spend her retirement years quietly.

That's when the trouble started. All of her possessions wouldn't fit in the apartment, and she refused to give them up. She had a veritable warehouse of Soviet crap, including 53 brand new berets, more shoes than Imelda Marcos, and what was probably the world's largest collection of metal serving trays with pictures of blood sausages on them. She had a mild nervous breakdown when the items went missing (stolen, she was convinced), and I tried to sooth her by replacing her black and white television whose Soviet-era antenna wouldn't plug into a modern socket. "Get out of here with that!" she screamed at me. "I like my television." But there were only two things important in her life: her Wednesday public sauna and any TV program starring Hannes Võrno, a local heartthrob. She finally agreed to take the new TV set only in the name of seeing Hannes.

Living in the new house, I soon learned that even her own family avoided her. She could be so hateful that her own two brothers refused to visit. So why was I so gullible?

After the TV episode, I tried to keep my distance from her, but she was unavoidable. She trapped me in her apartment — which reeked of grilled fatback and rabbit shit — and shouted me down if I tried to interrupt her discourses on the best open air markets for buying pig tails. She would also demand I recharge her telephone card and then verify I'd done the job right by dialing 112, the local version of 911. "Sorry, wrong number," she giggled like a child making a prank call, as soon as the emergency operator picked up. She would call me down to fix her TV remote, and I would clean out the food stuck between the buttons with a wet cloth and readjust the antenna. It was on one of those days, bent down behind the TV set, that I noticed her rabbit had eaten through the electrical cords. I told her the rabbit would have to go and she brushed me off. "He only chews through the small cords," she said. "That's not dangerous."

"What about this big fat cord I'm holding in my hand?"

"The builder did that! He's always scraping things!" The week before, she had told the builder that I was plotting to kill her. I didn't know what to do. I thought of asking

Hannes Võrno to stop by and say something nice on my behalf.

I took out a classified ad and arranged for the rabbit to have a good home in the countryside, replete with green pastures and happy children. The day the rabbit's new family arrived to get him, I asked them to wait behind the gate while I went to get the rabbit. The aunt first refused to believe the rabbit had to go. I mentioned the electrical cords. She denied it. I gave her a cross look, and she told me to turn off the electricity in her apartment. "I don't need it. I'd rather have my rabbit than electricity!" There was nothing else to do but take the rabbit.

She pulled from her side, and I pulled from mine. She screamed. I swore. The cage separated into pieces and the rabbit scrambled for cover. As she cried, I quietly gathered the creature by the ears and took it out to its new family.

Why did I have to deal with a nutty old woman whose own family wouldn't talk to her? Why was this *my* problem? Feeling guilty over the rabbit affair, I asked Liina that very question.

"Just why do you?" she replied.

I guess I felt sorry for the old gal. And because I was thousands of miles from my own family, and because I craved for a deeper connection to my new home than a stamp in a passport could provide. I was trying to be a part of the family I'd inherited. But I should have been smarter. Had I paid a little more attention I would have noticed there was good reason her own family had abandoned her. Had I planned a little bit, I could have found a better defense. I could have pretended to be deaf or to not speak Estonian.

What happened to the aunt after the rabbit left her? Nothing, really. We got her a dog the next week, and she hasn't mentioned the rabbit since. She still tells whoever will listen that I'm trying to kill her, but then she still begs me to come down and clean the food out of her remote control. I guess that means we're back to where we started. Which perhaps isn't a bad place to be.

❷ What Hemingway Said

Estonians are fond of quoting Hemingway: "In every port in the world, at least two Estonians can be found." I was fairly well informed about Hemingway, but I'd never heard that before I first came to Estonia. Visiting the United States, I tried out the quote on an officer of the Hemingway Society. He shot me a look like I'd asked something petty, like what brand of deodorant Hemingway used. "I don't believe Hemingway remarked on Estonia," he sniffed. "But I suppose it's possible. Hemingway said a lot of things."

A few years later, an Estonian magazine editor pointed out the specific passage in *To Have and Have Not*. Needless to say, I was a bit embarrassed by my own ignorance, as well as that of the Hemingway Society man. But, in fairness, perhaps it's not right to expect an academic to know every sentence from every Hemingway book. Especially when the phrase comes from a book that Hemingway himself is said to have called "junk." And if we want to split literary hairs, the Estonian-language version of Hemingway isn't exactly accurate. Still, these are all excuses. The fact is: Hemingway wrote about Estonians.

Estonians may be tempted to scoff at the ignorance of North Americans, but better they use it to their advantage. Despite Hemingway's contribution, Estonia is so little known you could say most anything and westerners would have to allow for its possibility. For example, Faulkner said that if he couldn't live in Mississippi, Estonia would have been his home of choice. James Joyce said that Estonians are better drinkers than the Irish—"and they know how to take a punch, too." Joseph Conrad lived on Tallinn's Vene Street for a few years, when he still went by the name of

Jozef Teodor Konrad Nalecz Korzeniowski.

Estonian taxpayers have spent millions behind the inane slogan, "Welcome to Estonia," but what the nation really needs are better storytellers. Who would better represent Estonia: an attractive but forgettable blonde who smiles and says "Welcome," or an "event of nature … face scarred by salt and burning wind … a statue sketched in a rough rock"? That's Hemingway in the words of Yevtushenko. And I didn't make that up.

Estonian President Toomas Hendrik Ilves strikes me as someone who has perfected the art of story telling about Estonia. I imagine him in his Columbia University days, in the darkest corner of an uptown bar, through a curtain of smoke from stinky European cigarettes, telling American coeds about his family's castle in Estonia. He would describe — with affected accent — the magnificent driven hunts where gentlemen afield drank claret from silver cups and his days riding a white steed through dewy fields to supervise serfs bringing in the harvest. That's an Estonian image to bring tourists. It's far more romantic than the actual toil and suffering. And it's far more compelling than "Welcome."

Several years ago Liina was on a Europe-bound flight with a CIA agent seated next to her. He was an advance man for John Ashcroft, preparing for the American Attorney General's visit to Moscow. The man claimed to be of Lithuanian origin. The agent was pleased to learn that Liina was Estonian, but as the conversation progressed, it became clear the agent knew very little about Estonia or Lithuania, either one. "Now just where is Estonia?" he finally asked.

Liina, not one to suffer the fool, answered with a deadpan "Africa."

"Of course Africa," replied the CIA man, "but where *exactly*?"

I've read that the Estonian government is preparing to spend over twelve million dollars over the next several years to promote Estonia's image abroad. I hope they'll release their inner storyteller and come up with something more riveting than "Welcome." After all, we've got all the props — castles, ruins, medieval cities — to stage a romantic play about dispossessed nobility. And if Estonians are reluctant to join in the production, perhaps President Ilves might agree to reprise some of the roles he used to play in that smoky corner of his favorite Manhattan bar? "Oh, yes, my dears, zis scar on my left cheek? It is from a duel with Vivonne de la Châtaigneraie, zee greatest swordsman of France…"

Estonians can put twelve million bucks behind saying "Welcome" if they want. But I favor crafting a story worthy of Hemingway. The West will swallow it whole. After all, Hemingway said a lot of things.

❸ Brothel Watch

Two years ago, a women's rights organization claimed there were sixty to one-hundred brothels operating in Tallinn, the capital of this former Soviet Republic. The police cracked down, and now it's believed there are only half that number. You can't deny the progress, but if you look at the numbers for very long (old or new, take your pick), you start to see brothels everywhere. You start to think your neighbors are operating bordellos. Which mine actually happen to be.

I live in Nõmme, supposedly one of the richest residential regions in the country. It's a small enough neighborhood that I know most foreign residents. At the beginning of last summer I heard English spoken on my neighbor's deck. They were just over the fence, through the hedge. The accents and voices changed daily, and it struck me as a very social family.

I wondered if I should I stick my head over the fence and introduce myself? "Hi, I'm Vello. Strange we haven't met before." But for some reason I didn't. Something held me back.

"It's probably a brothel," my wife Liina said.

"In this neighborhood?" I said. "You must be kidding."

"There's one up by the petrol station which they just closed. They're all over."

A week later, I ordered a taxi and got a driver who liked to talk. He was seventy years old, had been driving since Soviet time.

"Lots of brothels in Estonia?" I asked. Why not ask? He would know.

"There were forty up until about a month ago," he answered, as naturally as if I'd asked about a football match. "But the police closed eight."

"What about in this neighborhood?"

"Oh, you've got two at least."

"The one near the petrol station," I said, trying to sound smart.

"And the one right behind you," he said. He named the address.

"Right," I said. "Of course." A guy can't admit to being too naïve.

Later on in the summer, when the apple trees were in full bloom, the brothel workers held a sing-along. Although the girls themselves were masked by the foliage, their voices carried throughout the neighborhood. It was like living next to a Girl Scout camp. And, I have to admit, they were pretty good.

Was this a practice to ready them for the workday? A friend suggested this was "the famous Estonian Whores' Choir," rumored to be competing with the Estonian Men's Choir for a shot at a Grammy. Whatever the reason, the ladies of the morning completed only two songs before disbanding to meet the challenges of the day.

Usually, though, the music isn't so pleasant. Most days are comprised of a mini Russian rock concert. The girls blast music as they hang red and black underwear out to dry on the balcony. Liina refers to the ritual as "raising the pirate flag."

"I wouldn't tolerate a whorehouse in my neighborhood," said a friend visiting from England. He was enjoying a drink in my garden with a group of friends, all of us listening to the cackle of a bleach-blonde and her john through the firs.

"I'd be afraid to complain," countered an Estonian. He suggested that the Estonian police — not always sterling examples of law enforcement — would reveal my identity to the hot-blooded types who own the brothel.

"You could call from a payphone," the Brit suggested.

"Yes, that might work," the Estonian agreed.

But I don't intend to call the police. Sure, the girls make too much noise, and maybe they do drive down the property value. But if the prostitutes were driven out, they might be replaced with worse. Like a family with teenagers. Teenagers with a rock band.

❹ Integrate Me

I was recently invited to speak to an English class comprised of all Russian students. From time to time, it's healthy to experience first hand the bitterness some young Russian speakers hold toward Estonians. This year's understatement: some don't like them very much.

It wouldn't have been so bad if they had disliked Estonians for the right reasons (headcheese, milk soup), but sadly, their understanding of Estonians was about as informed as Borat's view of the Jews. And not even half as funny.

I don't know if the class was representative of Estonia's larger Russian population, but there were ten kids, seven of whom claimed to speak Estonian. The three who did not were the most bitter. All ten, though, said they did not interact with Estonians on a daily basis, except in forced environments.

The kids who didn't speak Estonian seemed to sit at home and wait for Prime Minister Andrus Ansip to personally appear and integrate them. They had no interest in learning Estonian and looked to the West — particularly the UK — as the land of opportunity. They thought it a place where they'd be received with open arms, paid well for having no education, and finally be treated as equals. "In Estonia," one told me, "if a Russian and Estonian are up for the same job and the Russian is more qualified, the Estonian still gets the job." I admitted maybe that was true, but that it wasn't only an Estonian phenomenon.

"If you and the girl on your right are up for a job in my country," I said, "and you're more qualified than she is, but she went to the boss' school, who gets the job?" He wasn't pleased to know that his superior CV might count for naught. And by the look on his face, I might have been the first to tell him that the world is unfair.

I don't know where he got this idea of England as paradise. Enough Russians have gone there and returned that accurate information ought to be available. But all the same, I tried to dismiss his misperceptions. He wasn't happy to hear that an Eastern European in England has to work twice as hard as any UK citizen. That he would be thought of as poor, dirty, and possibly a criminal — the very same words he used to describe how Estonians perceive Russians.

I made little progress if any. What can you do with angry kids? Their teacher told me it was pointless to argue; they just needed someone to listen, and they'd turn out all right. I hope he's right. I can't be so optimistic. A sixteen year-old ethnic Russian who speaks not a word of Estonian? Who thinks the West is going to welcome him?

I hope the kid gets his ticket West soon. Because the sooner he figures out that the world owes him nothing, the sooner he'll get to start making up for lost time.

But. There's always a but: Estonians could go easier on him.

If there's a period of history when only Estonians lived in Estonia and the Estonian language was spoken by all, I haven't heard of it. Some, who like to talk about the "good old days," have painted Tallinn as an "Estonian city" during the country's first independence. But Russification of Estonia has been around a long time, and according to historian and former Prime Minister Mart Laar, half of Tallinn spoke Russian in 1917. It doesn't take high science to know that no amount of legislation, policy, or wishful thinking is going to make a young Russian speak Estonian if he doesn't want to learn. The more laws you pass, the more he'll hate you.

He's got to want it naturally, which is what the free market is for. When the better jobs go to Estonian speakers, there's motivation to learn the language. It of course won't happen overnight — but it can and is happening as you read this. Many of my Russian friends and acquaintances speak Estonian. Most better than I do.

In the meantime, while we non-Estonians are attempting to integrate, the government could call off its dogs. Raids by the language inspectorate on trade schools where teachers of auto mechanics don't speak Estonian is a pointless and heartless exercise. It's like beating up your neighbor's grandmother just to show you can. Nobody's impressed, and you piss off the neighbors for no real gain. (Yes, I understand the need for some legislation to guide the market. But sometimes those charged with enforcement are like teenagers with the keys to dad's car: they can't resist seeing how fast it will go.)

Is the Estonian language in critical danger? There were once three hundred Native American languages spoken in North America. Now, two-thirds of them are lost. Another died recently with Marie Smith Jones, the last living speaker of Eyak. But the fact that Estonian has been kept alive two thousand years suggests Estonians may know something Native Americans do not.

If the Estonian language is well-looked-after enough to survive one more generation, what's the harm in the language inspectorate turning a blind eye now and again? Give ethnic Russians a reason to like you, and let the market do its work. I can't recall the last time I saw an ad in the newspaper which read: *Wanted: Uneducated ethnic Russian with visible chip on shoulder.*

There's clear advantage to learning Estonian. My friend from the English class may not yet see it, but most do. If we stop beating up granny, I believe all but the most hopeless will eventually come around. And if they don't — well, there's always England.

⑤ Cock Ring Ken

There's a conspiracy afoot.

The door on my brand new Samsung washing machine didn't close properly and leaked water all over the floor. My Nardi refrigerator — also purchased new — made a noise like an incoming mortar round and we had to call customer service immediately. "Oh, these all have that problem," shrugged the repairman, as if the greater part of his work was following brand new appliances from the showroom to the customer's home. Last week, I bought a new Samsung telephone. Broken, of course. Everyone who called me complained of an echo.

Sometimes, especially during a long streak of cold, gray days, I am convinced of a conspiracy. I imagine manufacturers' warehouses full of defective appliances awaiting shipment to Eastern Europe where many customers haven't yet a clue they're supposed to be king. Does this, in fact, happen?

In 1993, the Mattel Company, maker of the universally popular Barbie doll, unveiled Barbie's new, updated boyfriend, Ken. The Ken doll sported an earring in his left ear, blond highlights in his traditionally brown hair, a purple mesh shirt, lavender vest, and a thick chrome ring worn on a necklace. The doll was officially named "Earring Magic Ken," but within weeks the world had dubbed him "Cock Ring Ken." Unwittingly, Mattel had made Ken gay.

A cock ring, for those of us who live outside the Barbie culture, is worn to trap blood in the penis and prolong an erection and orgasm. Almost immediately, kitsch-minded gay men gobbled up Cock Ring Ken making it the best-selling Ken doll in the company's history. Mattel denied emphatically that Ken was gay — "We're not in the business of putting cock rings into the hands of little girls," said a company spokesman — and argued that the cock ring was, in fact, a "circular charm." The company discontinued and recalled the doll.

Or did they?

In 1994, I walked into the toy department of the state department store in Tartu, the country's second largest city, and found the shelves packed with the purple-shirted Cock Ring Ken. There were hundreds of frosty-haired twelve-inch boxed homosexuals gazing out into the aisle. I don't have trouble imagining the conversation in the Mattel boardroom.

"Let's burn them."

"No, then we'll be called fag haters."

"Hey, let's ship them to Estonia and sell them there!"

"Estonia? Never heard of it."

"Exactly!"

To be fair, I doubt citizens of Tartu were the only consumers blessed with a shipment of Cock Ring Ken. He was probably sent all over Eastern Europe. But if any once-upon-a-time little girl from Tartu reading this thinks she may have a Ken doll somewhere in the closet, I suggest she go take a look. Cock Ring Ken does a bustling business on eBay.

But my conspiracy theory goes beyond toy companies.

The Estonian military, for many years, was the West's charity case and received their old, run-down vehicles. The Estonian National Guard received WWII-era Swedish bicycles. Their usefulness wasn't quite apparent to anyone. "If war breaks out," a guardsman told me, "then I'll drive to Tartu and assemble my bike."

I don't have an elaborate plan to end Estonia's status as the dumping ground for the West's old or defective products. I have a simple plan. Never accept second best when paying full price. But, as they saying goes, people treat you like you treat yourself. Estonians have to start demanding their rights as consumers.

One of my colleagues recently invited me to the office parking lot to witness the job Peugeot had done on her car. A minor accident necessitated the painting of her car's trunk, and the dealer had painted it a different color than the rest of her car. She complained, and after several grunts of protest, the dealer relented and agreed to do the job right. But she had to wait two weeks. His guys were busy fixing other cars.

What should she have done? In some cases, and this is one of them, physical violence is an appropriate response. Had she immediately grabbed the dealer by the testicles and forced him to endure a short speech about common sense, good manners, and the general rights of human beings not to be made fools of by car dealers, I think any good judge would have let her off without even a fine. It would have been a clear case of self-defense.

In the name of consumer rights, I've started to ask probing questions when purchasing appliances. "How many of these refrigerators are broken?" I asked a salesman just last week. "Sir," he replied, "we sell *new* appliances." I then related my story of the Great Conspiracy. I told him about useless bicycles, bad paint jobs, and, of course, the detailed saga of Cock Ring Ken. He studied me for a long time before replying.

"So you think these refrigerators might be gay?"

That wasn't my thought exactly, but I had to admit he might be right.

❻ Baltic Banking:
The Good, the Bad, and the Ugly

Hansabank doesn't object to your business, but they don't seem to want it, either. In the early 1990s, I was a private banking customer, and they were always glad to see me. My personal banker was dazzlingly good — better than any banker I've ever had in Canada or the US. No kidding.

But in the late '90s, I left Estonia, and they ceremoniously stripped me of my private banking status, cutting up my pearl-level debit card, so that I wouldn't give it to a friend to get free parking behind the bank. But I understand. My salary left the country with me, so what was the point in keeping me?

Several years ago, I returned, and Hansa asked me to rejoin them in private banking. I demurred, pointing out that my asset base was far below the one-hundred-thousand dollars they required, and that I didn't have plans to earn great sums of money. "That's okay," they said, "You might take a home loan from us." *Might* is the word, I said. No promises.

A month later, a Hansabanker called and explained in Pidgin English that I was being kicked out of private banking. "But why'd you take me in the first place?" I asked.

"Probably mistake," she said. "I don't know. I just have to call you."

Fair enough. She could have taken a lesson in diplomacy, but her English was rotten, so I forgave.

A month later, I applied for a loan. To their credit, they cut through all the formalities immediately, allowing me to put the loan in my name instead of my Estonian wife's. Hansabankers are practical professionals. From a North American perspective, their loan offer was good — interest rate competitive, origination fee fair. I was ready to sign.

But then SEB called. They asked me if I wouldn't stop through, have a cup of coffee, to just see if they might have a chance. To any human being, that has real appeal. *You don't have to fill out any of our 143 stupid, repetitive forms; just drop by.* Within minutes, they'd pulverized Hansabank's offer. They simply wanted my business. I thanked Hansa for their work and signed with SEB.

There are some things I've always found strange about SEB. For starters, their main office is a black spike violating the sky, the Darth Vader of Tallinn buildings. Inside, it's like a Las Vegas casino. Tellers are circled like blackjack dealers with supervisors behind them like pit bosses. And the tellers wear polyester. I'd rather die than wear flammable clothing.

But none of that stopped me. Despite their Vegas trappings, they seemed easy enough to work with. They were entirely flexible. I liked them a lot.

Then Sampo Bank called. They were so late with their offer that I'd forgotten I applied there. As far as banks go, Sampo is probably the warmest. They occasionally play Latin music in the lobby, and their employees are the most likely to smile (perhaps because, of all Estonian bank uniforms, theirs least resemble McDonald's).

But despite the fact that I liked Sampo, they offered diabolical loan terms. They were willing to finance my house, but would write contracts only as long as my residence permit was valid. If it ever wasn't renewed, they would call the note immediately. I'd already signed with SEB, but I was still curious why they'd set such a condition. "You could flee the country, and we'd have nothing," the banker said.

"But the property's going nowhere," I said. "And I own it outright."

"Still, you could flee the country." SampoMan was a broken record. He was just parroting the deep thinkers on his loan committee.

In the name of research, I decided to swing by Nordea Bank. Stuck across the lobby from the Palace Hotel bar, Nordea resembles a gypsy camp: it might pick up and move at any moment.

"Can I help you?" a woman asked, peering out from behind the partition on her desk after I'd shuffled my feet a bit to announce my presence.

"Curious about home loans," I said.

"Fill these out," and she pushed a sheaf of papers my way.

"Actually, I have some rather unusual circumstances ..."

"Fill these out." She slapped a pen on the pile.

I took the pile and gave them a once-over. The whole thing felt distinctly governmental. "I think I'll complete these at home," I said, stepping back into the Palace lobby, depositing the forms in a trash can. Nordea's not much of a bank, I thought. But you do have to ask yourself: how many banks are so close to a Jack Daniel's on the rocks?

❼ Spies Like Us

My friend's father is convinced I'm CIA. I've been here close to fifteen years and, despite Tallinn's wonderful weather, he can't see why any married man would stick around here that long. Maybe I am CIA. Maybe you are, too. But whether I'm a spook or not, I've certainly heard a lot of good spy stories about Estonia.

In the early 1990s, it was said Chinese spies were operating out of Tallinn's only Chinese restaurant, because the Estonian government wouldn't allow them an embassy. The story went that some Estonian guy had visited China as part of a government delegation and been given a Chinese spy to shadow him while he was here. When this Estonian guy went to eat in Tallinn's Chinese restaurant three years later, guess who his waiter was?

About the same time, another story circulated that the US government sent spies to Estonia with suitcases of cash in order to buy big Estonian businesses, from which they'd have an inside track on Estonian goings-on and good reason to meet with government. Nice work if you can get it. I'd have bought the brewery.

There was also the story about an American embassy worker who used to get drunk and accost expatriates in bars, paralyzing them with fear by reciting their names and the names and ages of their children.

And of course they used to say that everyone at the Russian embassy was a spy. Maybe they were. Maybe they still are. I've heard the same about the Americans.

If you want to have fun with American embassy workers (at social functions away from their bullet-proof glass), extend your hand and when they introduce themselves you say: "Ah, of course. I remember you from Langley." Or you can strike up a conversation about the firing range in the embassy cellar or the AV-8B Harrier parked on the roof. These are always interesting topics.

I once made friends with an American embassy worker and then raised the issue at a noisy party where I was sure the Russkies couldn't eavesdrop. "So who are the spooks in the embassy?" She was taken aback — I guess that's not a common question she received at formal receptions. "Oh, come on," I said, "there must be at least one." She paused a minute to compose herself — calling on her Langley training, no doubt — and answered that if there were any she wouldn't know them. "Even the ambassador wouldn't know," she said. I found that hard to believe and said so. But she told me that if there were any spies, they'd most likely be top men in the business community. "Or journalists," she added. "Like you."

A Russian military friend once told me a story about an American spy. The US government was in need of a super spy and it searched all over America, finally finding the perfect candidate at Harvard University. They took him to Langley, taught him hand-to-hand combat, weaponry, driving skills, languages — all what spies need. Then they gave him a parachute and dropped him out of the sky over Siberia, where he made his way to a small village and infiltrated the community. After he'd been there about six months, there was a great party, where everyone was far drunker than usual. "Say," a villager said to the spy, "there's something I've been wanting to ask you." The spy said to fire away. "You're a great guy," said the villager. "And your Russian is perfect. You make the best *pelmeni* I've ever had, and you're by far the best balalaika player in the village. But tell me one thing: What's a black guy doing in the middle of Siberia?"

Not exactly flattering. But after the great CIA work in Iraq, it's entirely believable.

I find it funny that my friend's father thinks I'm CIA. Why wouldn't he think I'm CSIS. (I'm Canadian, after all.) The reason he doesn't think I'm CSIS is because he's never heard of it. That's just how super secret it is. We keep a low, low profile. We're so deep undercover you've never heard of us.

I've also met with the Estonian intelligence service, KaPo. They've got a cool sounding name, which belies their tiny operational budget. They don't have many cool James Bond toys, either. Skype employees have better. But the KaPo agents I've met were very professional, and I have a lot of respect for them. Personally, I think to make up for their budget, and in the name of NATO friendship, the US should allow them to use the embassy's firing range or their Harrier jet. But that's just the opinion of a friendly, sharing Canadian.

From the vast knowledge about espionage I've demonstrated here, you've probably concluded I'm CSIS. I can't tell you, of course. Or, as they saying goes: I could tell you, but then I'd have to kill you. But if you do think I'm a spy, do me one favor. Don't mention CSIS. It's an awful name, one so clunky no one would be proud to work there. Instead, use the organization's French name: *Service canadien du renseignement de sécurité*. That's a name I can be proud of. And it's a name any Estonian Bond girl would fall for.

⑧ Love Thy Neighbor

My wife and I used to rent a house next door to a brothel where, weather permitting, the prostitutes would come out and sing on the porch. They could carry a tune pretty well. It was a tough neighborhood to leave, all that excitement just twenty meters outside my door. But the rent was high and the place poorly insulated, so we moved out. Luckily, our new neighborhood isn't a total bore.

The kid next door regularly disassembles his entire car, strewing the parts all over his yard, and puts it back together within a couple of hours. I've often wondered if he's training to work in a Formula One pit crew. Or perhaps he wants to be a deejay. During his automotive work, he shares his music with the entire neighborhood: Imagine the sound of an aquarium's oxygen pump set to a heavy drum beat with the voice of a tortured dog. All this at a concert-level 120 decibels. Looped. But he's not a bad kid. He borrowed my ladder one day and brought it back. He loaned me his dad's garden hose.

Another neighbor hosts Tallinn's taxi drivers. Every few minutes one departs from his house and another arrives. So many taxi drivers in one place make me nervous. I've convinced myself the house is either a drug den or the local headquarters for Russia's *Nashi*. There might even be some WMDs inside.

There's also an elderly woman who likes to garden in the vacant lot next to our house. The builders plowed it under months ago, readying it for construction, but she's still out there trying to save the poppies that grew before the demolition. I once saw her waiting for a bus, took her aboard my car, and she remarked: "Oh, so chivalrous. You treat me like a German lady." She sometimes leaves nasty notes for us on the fence, telling us to replace her flowers or fix her clothes line, the former which we haven't touched, the latter which hasn't existed since the lot was plowed under.

But I'm sure our neighbors aren't in love with us, either. My wife's aunt, who lives below us and is not fully sane, dries her laundry on the fence, making our garden look like a gypsy camp in a yuppie neighborhood. She also exercises her rabbit in the yard, and squeals for hours in a high pitch when it escapes under the fence. But she won't allow me to build a hutch for it. "He wants to be free," she screamed at me. "Can't you see he wants the whole garden?"

The outside of our house is awaiting its final coat of paint. Due to a major mistake by the builder, the house looks like it's suffering from a skin disease, and the banker next door keeps asking when we're going to finish it. "We're all out of money," I say. "But I do hope to complete it before I die." Actually, the builder has sworn he'll fix it within the month. But no point me telling the banker that.

It's never easy being a good neighbor. It's even harder when you're in a culture not your own, surrounded by people you think are complete crackpots. But I know that's what they think of me, too. And so while we may not be the best of friends, at least there's comfort in knowing we're even.

⑨ Your Friendly Neighborhood UFOnaut

L ately, I've been haunted by silence.

Shopping at Selver, my local supermarket, I was troubled by the silent treatment from my checker. I offered a hello, which was met by nothing at all. She continued to drag items across the scanner, very much like the store's recycling machine that takes my empty beer cans. Except the recycling machine speaks, a soft gurgling sound as the cans are sucked through the chute.

In the presence of others, too much silence bothers me. I'm from a culture of idle conversation. I'm used to hearing about the checker's grandkids, the deer her husband shot this season, or her thoughts on local politics. Small talk which over time amounts to something more. But the Selver checker made no sound.

A visiting friend once asked me what the Estonian words for "please" and "thank you" were. I quipped that it didn't matter, since no Estonian used them, anyway. Liina didn't find it funny and tried to argue that Estonians are friendly people. If that's true, then they're the only people who show it by not talking to you.

To prove my point (to myself; no point arguing with Liina), I decided to go a full week without speaking to any Estonian I didn't know, except for bare minimum phrases like "bus ticket" or "large beer." For the first few days, I fancied myself a Marie Curie. I was advancing the frontiers of science through daring personal experiments.

But by the fifth day, I was utterly depressed. I couldn't cope with how smoothly things had gone. Checkers were not remotely bothered by the fact that I didn't talk. Most perfunctorily asked if I had a Partner Card and accepted my silence as a no. A few did say hello, but these were obviously trained by someone like Peep Vain, the Estonian Anthony Robbins, so many years ago that their greeting had long lost its shine. I could even sense their relief when I failed to answer. "Thank God," meant their exhaled breath, "I may now return to my own private world."

But while the checkers were happy, I was despondent. I realized I could go my entire life in Estonia without talking, and it would not upset the delicate balance of things. I also began to feel a bit self-conscious. In America, someone who walks around in complete silence would be thought a child molester. My quiet self made me nervous.

After a week of silence, I needed a change. As a man of science, I decided to reverse my experiment: I would be conspicuously friendly to checkers. I would learn where their grandkids went to school. I'd ask how venison tasted. I'd ask if they thought Minister Reiljan was guilty of taking bribes.

I arrived in line with enthusiastic "good mornings" and departed with sincere "good days." I didn't leap to the grandkids right away, but started gently, calling attention to dreadful weather, to the rise in price of potato chips. A very few warmed to me, but most ignored me or twisted their faces, wondering what sort of UFOnaut had landed in front of their cash registers.

For a while, my enthusiasm overflowed into other areas of my life. Not only was I greeting checkers, I was nodding and smiling to people I didn't know as I passed them on the street. Occasionally, a pretty girl would smile back, but most screwed their faces groundward and walked on, probably wondering if I wasn't some sort of child molester.

I've since ended my experiments and tried to revert to the real me. I'm sometimes silent, sometimes outgoing, but usually I'm somewhere in between. While standing in line at Selver, I often find myself thinking back to my Toronto childhood. There was a mentally retarded kid who lived in my neighborhood, and he spent his days roaming the streets, doing nothing else but flashing a toothy grin and waving to everyone he encountered. People thought he was an UFOnaut. But thinking back, he was, without a doubt, the happiest person in the neighborhood.

①⓪ A Domesticated Imperialist

'**N**ow Riga, that's where?" My two American guests who landed at the Tallinn airport had seen nothing of Estonia and were already asking about further adventures. "Latvia? Is that a different country? Does it have its own money?" I confirmed that Latvia indeed had its own money. Estonia, too, I said. "You mean they don't take dollars here?" they asked incredulously. "They take dollars in Mexico."

The Americans had a hard time understanding they weren't in Mexico. *Dónde está* … they tried with Tallinners but were met with blank looks. They had a hard time understanding they weren't in Russia, too. "You mean Estonia isn't part of Russia?" I heard one guest's friend ask via the Skype phone in my living room. "No," my guest shouted back into the microphone, "but I had thought so, too."

Proper nouns were impossibly difficult for them. Jaanika became Jana. Monika was shortened to Mona. Roosi turned to Rosa. And they never got Mare right. It was always Mora. City names were too much, too. Stockholm was Stockton, perhaps because of California. Ahvenamaa, where they planned to visit via ferry, was known — without a trace of irony — as *Antenna maa*.

I showed them Tallinn's medieval Old Town, but they were unimpressed. It was impossible for them to enjoy, because everything was a competition: "Our streets are wider than yours. Our cars are bigger than yours. American women have bigger breasts." The only thing that really impressed them was the Soviet housing development, Lasnamäe, with its miles of identical concrete apartment blocks. They stood next to my car, mouths agape. It was the only time during the trip they weren't talking. After a few minutes of wonderful silence, one remarked, "They must have a real problem with gangs here, but I don't see any graffiti." I tried to explain that the apartments were inhabited by nice, normal people, most of whom didn't rape and murder for a living. But the Americans weren't listening. They hovered close to the car and snapped photos.

They took a lot of photos during the trip, ninety-five percent of them from the car window. One of the guests was grossly overweight, and he was unaccustomed to walking any distance greater than from his sofa (electric-powered recliner model with remote control) to the refrigerator (five temperature zones plus icemaker). Both had trouble getting in and out of my European-made car, and the larger guest talked repeatedly about the diesel two-ton pickup he owned. "It's like a Cadillac inside."

What struck me most wasn't their ignorance — ask me questions about a small, far-off land, say Switzerland, and I can't answer them — but their complete lack of interest in learning. When I wasn't around to serve as a personal guide, they sat in front of the television. "Now, what language is this one?" they asked Liina. "Finnish? That's a language? Where do they speak that? Why can't you get CNN?"

The average American views the world through a single lens. He too often assumes the world is Christian and white and that everyone speaks English (okay, a few speak Mexican). Except for loving God, Americans love freedom above all. And if other cultures don't love freedom, it doesn't matter, because God loves freedom, and if God loves freedom you will, by God, eventually love it, too.

An Estonian friend of mine, one who often seems to play the role of my older brother, refers to me as the Domesticated Imperialist. I'm still part of a hegemonic culture, he knows, but he believes living in Europe has smoothed some of my rough edges. I've attempted to abandon my American habit of asking everyone's name and what each does for a living. When meeting new people, I try to remember not to always offer my hand. And I am trying to learn to listen. It isn't easy, of course. There's something in the genetic code of imperialists which requires us to talk. To share our knowledge. To help others. To help you.

And who doesn't want to be helped?

❶❶ And Nice to Meet You, Too

My first instinct was to be angry with my wife for not introducing me. Second, I thought I might introduce myself, but they already somehow knew me, my name, my connection to the few I knew in their group. They even made me feel like I should know their names. They asked me polite questions: "So, you're back for good in Estonia?" "How's the job working out?" There were eight of them at the table, only three of whom I knew. And one of the three was my wife.

Perhaps atypical of Estonian dinner parties, the conversation — on their part — flowed. But I couldn't take part. I could only sit and wonder: *Who are you people?*

I had more questions, too. What do you do? What is your connection to everyone else at this table? And how in hell do you know me?

But I didn't ask. I didn't want them to think I was an American. The type who'll pry with invasive questions. The American style of questioning can go out of control, the asker soon demanding to know what kind of car they drive, how much money they earn, and which celebrities they've slept with.

I know it's not the Estonian custom to be known. Some say this is a Finno-Ugric trait. Some say it's Soviet. My theory is that breaking bread in Estonia is not a grave enough act to warrant introductions. Despite the trappings of modern dining, food is fuel, and even if we were eating seven courses, somewhere deep in the Estonian soul a peasant voice is urging them to hurry back into the fields.

I often think Estonians want to introduce themselves but are too shy. So they employ subtle tactics. "My name is Eed," said one at the table. "People think it's a man's name. I get lots of mail addressed to Mr. Eed..." I like to think that Eed sensed my discomfort and found a clever way to introduce herself, without derailing a thousand years of Estonian dining tradition.

As an outsider in this country, I try to accept the folkways without question. I will nip from the community bottle. I will tie the string and nail around my belt at a wedding. Were I to worry over introductions too much, the question would cease to be *Who are you?* and become *What's wrong with you?*

Still, I sit frustrated. In my head, I have prepared the full text of a speech on the importance of dining. I imagine rising from my chair, throwing down my napkin, and citing examples from the world's dining history. Jesus knew the names of his twelve guests. Ovid's Olympian gods were acquainted. Bartenders at the Folies-Bergère knew dozens.

At the end of the evening, after much discomfort, I resorted to my first instinct and got angry with my wife. In the car, I told her if she wanted me to come to any more dinner parties, she'd better introduce me to the people I didn't know.

"But I didn't know them either," she said.

I sat in silence, brooding.

"Oh, there was that one," she said. "I think her name was Eed."

❶❷ Aboard the Vomit Comet

W hen I was a kid, a friend of mine had a t-shirt which read, *Beer: Breakfast of Champions.* Now, thirty years later, I took a cruise with the Estonian company Tallink and realized the words on the t-shirt weren't a joke. In fact, my wife Liina suggested they could even be Tallink's slogan.

We were aboard the *Romantika*, sailing for Sweden, home of what are known in Canada to be clean, pristine, well-mannered Scandinavians. I expected a boat full of smiling blondes in cable-knit sweaters, hands still creamy from churning butter by hand and yodeling tunes from *The Sound of Music* against a sunny, mountainous backdrop. But instead, I got vomit.

If a reader believes I may be inclined toward poetic license and manufacture such details, he may verify my story by checking the Tallink terminal cleaning log. *March 24th, 17:10 hours: One large vomit pie directly inside the terminal's main entrance.* If Tallink doesn't keep such logs, I may be persuaded to share my high-resolution photograph.

My party advanced to the *Romantika*, and we sailed without further incident. I soon convinced myself that if I'd had my Miami CSI junior crime lab kit with me, I'd have been able to conclude that the vomit inside the terminal was not from a passenger aboard my ship. Chemical analysis would prove it to be vomit of Finnish origin.

The Swedish passengers, however, failed to meet my expectations. I saw no cable knit and very few smiling blondes. Youngsters wore jeans slung low like wannabe gangsters from an American MTV video, and their shaggy-dog haircuts reminded that Sweden is a country where the 1970s never died.

But children and adults alike were painstakingly courteous, and the usual elbowing for a place in the buffet line was replaced by *"after you's"* and offers to cut an extra piece of bread for the next passenger. We all simply lined up and ate. It was all too civilized.

Fortunately, I was seated at a table with a former officer of the cargo vessel *Sigulda*, who regaled us with tales of sailing under the Soviet flag to Beirut in 1979. The city burned, half-sunken ships smoked in the harbor, and yet the good ship *Sigulda* sailed on through dangerous waters to deliver her cargo to the citizens of Beirut.

"What were you carrying?" asked Liina.

"Laundry detergent," replied the officer.

"Then you're a hero."

"Indeed," laughed the officer. "Nothing like detergent to clean up after a war."

The officer told more stories. He told us how the Estonian ship *Georg Ots* carried Gorbachev to the Iceland Summit. How Gorbachev traveled with his personal chef, wine collection, and seven kinds of imported cheese for breakfast. He talked about the good old days when working on a cruise vessel was a rare privilege and the crew stood shipshape in starched shirts and creased pants.

But aside from the excitement the officer provided, there wasn't much action to be found on the boat. In the absence of drunken cruising Finns to wrestle with, we had to manufacture our own fun.

Liina and a friend went to the ship's makeup store where they amused themselves by applying too much rouge and coloring their eyelids bright blue. Resembling circus clowns, they approached Estonian shopgirls and asked in Russian, *"Krassivuiye, da?"* The shopgirls, not too convincingly, agreed they were stunning.

A Swedish passenger, seeing the girls in an early stage of makeup application, took Liina for the ship's makeup consultant, and asked her for advice. "Bright and shiny always beautiful," replied Liina in heavy Russian-accented English. "Pretty woman reflect light like mirror."

The officer and I remained in the restaurant, autographing the wine bottles they leave on tables with our best rendition of *Toomas Hendrik Ilves*. We tried out the only Swedish we knew on the waiter: *Hüür monga elefanten här dü homma?* If I understood correctly, the waiter responded that he had no elephants at home and that the Estonian president's signature on a wine bottle did not, in fact, make it more valuable.

Stockholm itself was uneventful. Everything was clean, the people polite, and city completely devoid of gunfights and car chases. There was good shopping, though. Except for public transport, everything was cheaper than in Tallinn. Flowers, clothing, even lunch in a tourist trap was cheaper. There were lots of savings, but not much excitement. We were glad to return to the ship.

The voyage home was in closer keeping with what I've come to expect from a Tallink cruise. A posse of Swedes celebrated their youth with mild rioting, tearing up and down through the ship's passageways all night long. No one slept, but then you're not supposed to on what is known in English as a booze cruise.

The next morning, the ship resembled Beirut as the officer had described it. Vomit and spilled drinks covered the floors of the passageways, food littered the carpet, and one area was flooded, thanks to a passenger who decided the ceiling fire extinguisher was optimally suited to hang clothing.

By the time we arrived in Tallinn, the crew had miraculously disinfected the hallways, repaired the flood damage, and made the ship vomit-free. The *Romantika* was about as romantic as it could ever get.

It's true what some Estonian politicians have said that Estonia is becoming just another boring northern European country. The Tallink cruises just ain't what they used to be. Of course it could be, too, that I'm just getting older.

❶❸ Across the Spanish Tomatoes

People stare at me in supermarkets. I don't know how many people read the Estonian weekly where my column appears, but many of its readers seem to shop where I do. They peer over fresh cabbage until their eyes meet mine. Then they glance downward, as if there were something on the floor they might buy.

I look like my photo in real life, though I've had my teeth fixed since then. Otherwise, I'm a readily identifiable average guy who's never had to deal with fame. I had one close call in Vancouver when my Esto-Canadian band, Reckless Dentistry, had a video on Much Music called "Passport for Grandma." We weren't as clever as we thought, and I wasn't much of a bass player. Rightly so, my fame was short-lived.

People have said I'm a better writer than musician, which I certainly hope is true. But as these columns become more popular, I'm not so sure I'm prepared for fame. And Estonian fame is of the strangest sort.

Andy Warhol said that everyone would be famous for fifteen minutes, but he never lived in a country that has fewer residents than his Manhattan neighborhood.

Curious about Warhol's prediction in an Estonian context, I turned to science. I pored over TV schedules to calculate that Estonia's three channels offer 1,450,800 broadcast minutes per year. Assuming the average Estonian lives 65 years, there will be over 94 million minutes of TV time to fill in a single lifetime. Divide by the Estonian-speaking population (a bit over 920,000), and every man, woman, and child will need to personally appear 102 minutes on local television stations. I imagine a never-ending episode of *Us*, Estonia's most popular talk show, hosted by a grating, nasal-toned white version of Oprah.

Scientifically-minded readers will find fault. Granted, broadcast minutes are sometimes filled with foreign programming. But in my favor, I did not include other mediums like radio, magazines, newspapers, and the internet. I also did not factor out infants, the elderly, and the indigent. If we adjust for those, the scenario is of a magnitude that would have frightened Mr. Warhol. Indeed, Estonians have a grim responsibility to feed the fires of fame.

Luckily, there are Estonians ready to unselfishly serve. Anu Saagim, Estonia's favorite media sex bomb, is one. When Anu runs out of something to say, she gets a tattoo or a breast implant or botox treatment, and then talks about that. When she's finally run the gamut of plastic surgeries and beauty treatments, it won't surprise me if she experiments with prosthesis. Who among us has not wondered which artificial leg boasts the sexiest curves?

Then there are three girls from the band, the Vanilla Ninjas. It's not my kind of music — though their English-language titles rival my band's "Passport for Grandma" — but those girls have done their national service by suffering through their fame. They flew to Iraq and sweated in body armor only to return home to the headline: *We plan to have kids at the same time.*

Politicians have it worse, though. When a politician's image appears on the TV screen, half of Estonia winces or spits. It's almost a national pastime to trash politicians. But since many of them deserve it, and because they're well paid, it's hard to pity them.

Fame even carries over into the foreign community. It is a fact that every foreigner who learns the Estonian language has gone on television to give an interview. They're never asked intelligent questions; rather they are invited before the klieg lights to scratch themselves like monkeys. Their role is to smile, butcher a few sentences, and show the Russian population that "See, it's not impossible to learn the language!" (Never mind that the Russian population doesn't watch Estonian television.)

I have a couple of friends who are famous Estonians. While the public generally respects their privacy — they're rarely hounded for autographs — I don't see the benefit of fame. The police won't fawn over you and tear up your speeding ticket: they're as likely to double-check the breathalyzer. Fame doesn't get you a better parking place or a better table in a restaurant, and it certainly doesn't get you money. I get stares in the grocery store but what I earn for my column remains a small constant. There are plenty of famous Estonians who lead middle-class or even below-middle class existences. What's the point in that?

It's too late to turn back now, but had I been smarter I would have used someone else's picture for my column. Someone who's already famous or would really like to be. However, if a certain amount of fame is the price for expressing one's views in the newspaper, I guess that's not an unfair bargain. But please do me one favor: Don't steal glances at me across the Spanish tomatoes. Come over and introduce yourself. We'll both have made a new acquaintance, and I won't feel half as awkward with my newfound fame.

❶❹ The Great Expert

I've heard it said countless times: Foreigners who live in Estonia are here because we can't get jobs in our own countries. We are, in a word, losers.

That's sometimes true.

I knew one guy who faked his entire background — fabricated a university education, work experience, even gave interviews on Estonian TV talk shows claiming to be a war correspondent. He talked about how he'd taken a sniper's bullet in North Africa, which he carved from his own leg with a rusty pocketknife on the battlefield before crawling through twenty kilometers of enemy minefields to safety. Later it was discovered he was a barber from Minnesota.

Another guy I know claimed to be an English count. He wore the same tweed outfit every day like he was on a driven hunt and liked to claim he'd taught Prince Harry to ride. He loved to play a pair of bagpipes for the Estonian press. Eventually, his ex-wife located him in Estonia and dispatched a brigade of lawyers. He owned a small bowling alley in Bristol and had neglected to pay his taxes.

Usually though, foreigners are not guilty of major fraud. Very few out-of-work British carpet layers claim to be heart surgeons. Few Ohio carpenters say they're the Buddha and start their own ashrams. Generally, foreigners don't even exaggerate their own abilities: rather they remain silent while Estonians do it for them.

In the 1990s, I worked for an Estonian advertising agency. I was often presented as a "great expert." True, I'd worked seven years in top agencies in Toronto and New York City, and I knew more about the subject than anybody in Estonia at the time, but I was far from a great expert. To be considered a great expert in North America requires a career of at least twenty years plus public accolade.

But can you blame me for remaining silent while being toasted as a great expert? What would have Estonians thought if I'd interrupted with, "Actually, I really don't know as much as you think…"? To say that would be out of character for a westerner. (That kind of modesty would be downright Estonian.)

Today, there are far fewer great experts around. In part, it's because many Estonians can claim fifteen years experience in business. Their confidence has risen and they're quicker to call bullshit when some foreigner starts spouting off about the proper way to do things. Nowadays, it's quite difficult for a foreigner to pull a rabbit out of hat. It's even harder for him to point to a cow and say it's a giraffe.

My educated guess is that only one in four foreigners in Estonia today is here because he's unemployable at home. Generally, his incompetence is so obvious that he can't get a job anywhere in the world. Those in that group do what they would have done at home: they get married, let the wife work, and sit on the couch and drink beer.

The rest of the foreigners here are adventurers, a little bit bored with all-too-predictable lives in their own countries.

The bad news is that the longer competent foreigners remain in Estonia, the less employable they are at home. After having worked in Estonian advertising a few years, I visited a headhunter in New York City. Strangely, she did not hail me as a great expert and did not throw rose petals or job offers at my feet. Rather, she looked me in the eye and said, "My god, Vello. Estonian advertising experience is the same as no experience at all."

Of course she was being an arrogant bitch — New Yorkers think their city is the center of the universe. But her larger point was that my Estonian experience was not of particular use in a market hundreds of times its size. "What are you going to teach Americans?" she asked. I wanted to answer "humility," but I resisted the urge.

Instead, I argued I was a great expert on cultures great and small. A nice, middle-class Canadian boy who understood complex consumer minds in cities as big as New York and countries as small as Estonia.

"Vello," she said. "Go back to Estonia."

And so I did. I know the longer I remain here the less qualified I am to work in my home country. Which is why I'm working hard to become the caliber of con man who can bullshit his way into a job anywhere in the world. I've tried to learn what I can from the American war correspondent and the English count. And my CV is looking pretty good. It reflects my years of experience as a best-selling writer, astronaut, judo champion, Formula One driver, CIA agent, astrophysicist, and Michelin-star chef. In fact, it's so good I'm having to trim it back: The Americans are starting to tell me I'm overqualified.

❶❺ The Best Man for the Job

I n Estonia, the best man for the job is a woman.

If you want to hire someone who'll show up on time, take pride in his work, solve problems before they arise, then don't hire him. Hire her.

The average young Estonian man has the grooming habits of a zombie. He appears mornings in the office having slept in his clothes. What was once a Caesar haircut has hardened to a protective crust. Dandruff carpets the shoulders of the dark suit he's never bothered to dry clean. His once-black shoes are gray and caked with debris from last night's party to celebrate the invention of the Zippo lighter.

Fashion-wise, he eschews a tie. Perhaps he sees himself as more the bank robber than the bank employee. Or perhaps he plans to join a British pop band. More likely, since he won't change clothes for the next 72 hours, he must be suitably attired for all activity. Milk the cow in the morning; go to work; go clubbing. He's a bit overdressed for the cow and a bit underdressed for the office, but neither party voices concern.

The average young man doesn't rate high in the savoir faire department, either. In job interviews he has the gall to ask about money before talking about the job itself. He begins with questions about what kind of laptop or ergonomic chair he'll get. "And my company car won't be Korean-made, will it? What's the mobile phone allowance? And can I have the chrome-plated model with the built-in laser pointer?"

He is manly to a fault. Like an American teenager, he likes to smoke and drink and "invest" in a car stereo worth more than his car. He loves to drive and can prove he's an excellent driver: "I can make it from Tallinn to Tartu in under an hour." He can also open a beer bottle with any object at hand. "Wanna see?"

Women are lesser creatures, and he would not be dissatisfied if Estonian women adopted the ways of the east and walked ten paces behind their men. Being lucky enough to live in a time of shrinking population, society allows him two or more families. And if family cramps his style, simply spreading his seed is accepted, too. Birth control is a woman's issue. He's just doing his job.

All the above considered, if you're in the hiring mode, who will you take? The woman, of course. She shows up on time for her interview, makes intelligent observations about your business, and doesn't put her feet on your desk even once. Her suit is appropriate and clean, and she rides the bus to work. Says she's never considered a car. She'd rather spend the money on her kids.

Of course not all Estonian men are such Neanderthals. My friend Jaanus has the manners of a Florentine Cardinal and dresses like an old world count. Most importantly, his behavior goes beyond mere studied manners: he shows deep, genuine consideration for others. This doesn't mean only stopping for pedestrians in crosswalks and holding the door for ladies — it manifests itself in small gestures too numerous to count. But Jaanus isn't the norm. He's a true gentleman, of which there are too few in any society.

It's the raggedy-assed multitudes we must improve. They're the ones we employ. The cogs in the ever-hungry European Machine. But as a society, we can't count on having women around forever to do our work for us. Women have babies, and many move out of the workforce to take on more important roles in the world. It's unfair to ask them to do the work of men, too.

For now, in Estonia, the best man for the job is a woman. Men take note. This is your wakeup call.

❶❻ He Who Would be Great Among You

On March 18th, I sat dumbstruck in the city council meeting room as the city's chief architect, Endrik Mänd, addressed Pirita residents who had come to discuss the zoning of their region.

When Mänd opened the meeting, he immediately put me on guard. My father, who served the city of Vancouver, once pointed out to me that "When there's only one microphone switched on in a meeting, then it's not a meeting; It's a lecture." And so it was with Mänd and his sidekick, Martti Preem. They sat on the dais, a full meter above everyone else, and spoke into a lighted microphone. Citizens were required to stand and shout, even though there were two microphones at every table. A lecture, indeed.

From their position on higher ground Mänd and Preem lobbed slights and indignities on the citizenry below. I paraphrase, but you get the idea:

"Well, what you say is true," was a canned Mänd response, almost his mantra, "but in the wider picture we've addressed it…"

But if they'd addressed it, a citizen pointed out, it wasn't reflected in the city's plan. "The plan on the screen is old," Mr. Preem fired back, "because the entire last month we spent answering your protest letters." The response letters the city sent — those I've seen — were all the same form letter, addressed to one person, with everyone else listed in the "cc" column. Busy, indeed.

Mänd scolded the public like children at one point, saying "…perhaps the citizens would like to do the planning themselves." Perhaps they would, indeed.

In general, it wasn't what was said but how it was said. Those on the dais seemed only present to humor the public, not to actually listen. The audience was but an unpleasant chore to be done away with quickly, much like poisoning rodents or cleaning dog shit off your lawn.

Across town, in Keila, something similar was happening. The city council, in an attempt to restructure the educational system, voted in late February to close two state schools and create one private school through a foundation. Like a vigilante cop, the council shot first and asked questions later: they made the decision without bothering to consult the parents' association of Keila Gümnaasium, the district's largest school. The trouble is: that's not the behavior of a lawman; that's the behavior of an outlaw. And the parents of Keila would simply like to be consulted before decisions are made about their children's education. Sounds only reasonable to me.

In the English language, the idea of "public service" gets a boost from its name. The word "serve" come comes from the Latin *servire*, which literally means to be a servant or slave. The entire idea of public service is, well, to serve. Nowhere in the word's etymology is there an evidence of a higher station in life (a dais) or a louder voice (microphone). It's about giving yourself to the people.

In Estonia, public servants work in "ametid." This has a less charitable root. *Amet* comes from the German, *amt*. In both German and Estonian, the word seems quite clinical and sterile, divorced from any connotations of service or responsibility toward the greater public good. An amet is nothing human. Rather, it's something an official can hide behind. Or use as a club. I'm not arguing that an *ametnik* can't serve the public good — there are some fine public servants in Estonia — but I am saying the title isn't the type to help remind a worker of his obligation to the public.

As I sat and listened to those opposed to the development of Pirita, I stood ready and waiting to hear from the other side. I waited and waited and then waited some more. But no one stood to support it. It's possible that absolutely no one supports it, except for the developer who stands to make a healthy profit. But he didn't need to show up, because it seemed he had the city to do his bidding. I'm sure I wasn't the only one wondering why that was.

Sadly, I'm not privy to the backroom dealings that determine the futures of Pirita and Keila. Nor am I in a position to understand the long reach of Estonia's party politics and financing as they pertain to local government. But I am in a position to understand basic good manners and respect toward citizens and taxpayers. Or the lack thereof.

Some of the best writing on public service is also some of the oldest. I like Matthew 20:26: "It is not this way among you, but whoever wishes to become great among you shall be your servant." The phrase is powerful: It is both a poetic rebuke of unhallowed ambition and a lodestar for those in public service.

The citizens of Tallinn deserve a lot better treatment by their public servants. I'm sure they're aware of that. I'm also sure they're not so naïve to think citing scripture is going to change things. The citizens are going to have to stand up for themselves during lectures. And refuse to sit down again until they get what they came for.

❶❼ Selling Salla: Finland's Dream for Russia

The Finns have done their part to develop the Salla border region as a Finnish-Russian tourist attraction. The Finnish side boasts ski resorts, visits with Santa Claus, wood sculpture competitions, ceramics, and reindeer petting zoos. But the Russians don't seem ready. The Finnish Commerce Tourism's English/Russian-language publication, *Salla Border*, tries to help, attempting to romanticize what Russia does have — "the Russia side of the border has a petrol station and duty free shop" — but the Russians don't seem eager to join the campaign. The truth be known, the petrol they sell contains water and the duty free shop's selection is worse than the tiniest Helsinki-Tallinn ferry.

But let's not sell Russia short. The Salla Border writers have overlooked the real jewel of the region: the Kandalaksha supermarket. Forget Tallinn, Finnish shoppers, this is where you go for bargains.

Like most things in Russia, it's not easy to find. If you stay alert on the road from Salla — the roads are so bad, there's little chance of falling asleep — look for it right after you pass under the railroad bridge. There's a sign on its concrete front with two thumbs up and text claiming "low prices" and "good quality." If you can't read Cyrillic text, look for the thumbs up.

Upon entry, a sober young man will closely scrutinize you. Large bags, cameras, anything big enough to hide a cucumber must be checked. This young man is firm but fair. Unlike in Soviet times, he won't force you to take a basket, and no one is required to wait in line. (In Soviet times, stores used the number of shopping baskets to regulate store traffic, customers without baskets standing in line to wait for someone to leave.)

Inside the store are stenciled signs, blue block Cyrillic on a white field. If you still can't find what you want, ask one of the many friendly clerks. They're the ones in green smocks and tall black hats like horsemen from the Caucuses. They'll personally escort you to the dairy section and provide advice concerning kefir. "This one's locally made," a clerk declared proudly. "That one, Aktiva, will keep you healthy." She refused comment on a third one made by Danone. There was also a refrigerator full of treats made from curds. These are marketed for children, but I bought a variety for the trip home.

Some things haven't changed since Soviet times, of course. Eggs still come straight from the chicken, unwashed, packed ten to a plastic bag. The meat looked suspicious, the Russians' idea of a butcher being any man with an axe and a tree stump. And the fish looked like someone had driven over it with a tractor before freezing it rock solid.

In some sections, Russian tradition and western marketing meet head on. Vodka, for instance. There were forty different brands. There was one with a camouflage label, Spetsnaz vodka, named for the Russian Special Forces commandos. "For strong people," the fine print read. There was every color of label and shape of bottle, the most expensive around five bucks per bottle. A friend picked one with a slick black label and English text. He held it up for examination. "That one's shit," said a passerby. My friend put it back.

At the checkout, scanners have replaced abacuses. Gone are the surly clerks who could move wooden beads at light speed, point at the wire and wood, and expect you to know how to read it.

In the car, on the way back toward Salla, I opened a coffee-flavored curd treat and settled back to reflect on Russia's consumer-friendly advances and prospects for the Salla region. But that didn't last long. No more than halfway into my treat, I was greeted by a long, thick black hair. My vision of the new, hygienic Russia was immediately replaced by an image of a toothless, cursing factory worker who had forgotten her hair net. I rolled down my window and flung the offending curd into the forest.

I wondered if maybe the Salla Border writers weren't right to confine their praise to the duty free shop and petrol station. People rarely complain about finding a hair in their gasoline.

①⑧ Letter from a Luddite

O ne of my colleagues, Matis, uses a Nokia Communicator E90. He says it's a 3G phone with MS Office compatibility, GPRS, WAP, wireless LAN, infrared Bluetooth, and "all communications protocols."

I have a blue telephone. It has an on-off switch on the top, and when I dial a number and push the green button, it will make a telephone call. I like this phone well enough, but I wish the battery would last longer than four calls. With Matis' help, I'm starting to check out new telephones.

We've visited several stores and gazed upon phones behind polished glass, displayed like diamond engagement rings in a Toronto jewelry store. Some of them cost as much as diamonds, too. I do my best to listen patiently while a salesman explains why a telephone is really worth 700 dollars. "But it's more than a telephone," the salesman senses my doubt. "It's a personal communications center!"

"A 'personal communications center?'" I ask. "Can it take a message?"

"Of course," sneers the little smartass.

"But can it send a fax?"

"Why would anyone want to send a fax?"

"I like faxes. I like to both send and receive them."

The young guy isn't certain if I'm serious. "Can it send a fax?" I repeat.

"No," he admits, scratching his head. "It cannot send a fax."

Matis shrugs apologetically to the salesman, as if to say "he's a crusty old fart." Which is true enough, I suppose. Matis is doing his best with me. But we're just two different breeds when it comes to tech.

Anytime Matis sees an ad for a new technology, he'll investigate it. Say they've added a ICBM function to his NORAD-rated GPS for his Subaru. Well, he's got to at least try it. All an advertiser needs to do is throw a new acronym in an ad, and within a week Matis will have such a well-informed opinion about it that he could write an article for *Consumer Reports*. And if he finds value in it — if it's "a powerful work tool," his favorite phrase — he'll soon have one on his desk.

Of course, it's not only Matis. It seems all Estonians love tech. I recently read a study which said Italians use mobile phones more than anyone else (to call their mothers) and then come Finns. Estonians have to be pretty close behind the Finns, because I see some of them making calls as early as seven a.m. (not to me, thank God).

So far, Matis hasn't been much help to me in finding a new phone — which in his world is called "hardware." In my world, I'm after a kind of simplicity Matis and most young Estonians can't begin to comprehend. I use a manual typewriter, fountain pen, and a Smythson Panama diary (the battery-free variety you write in with a pencil).

I've about given up on Matis' ability to help me with a phone and am starting to fly solo, checking out ads for new phones on the market. I'm looking for that just-right phone which will fit into my Luddite world, one that is simple to use and won't require a weeklong NATO training course.

I've noticed a Samsung ad urging me to "improve my business image." Not for me, as I don't have a business image. And the guy in the ad looks exactly like the Brylcreem man from 1970's advertising. Brylcreem was the gel which turned gray hair black and helped old guys get chicks. "A little dab'll do ya," they used to say. It's possible the 1970's Brylcreem man appeals to some, but he strikes me as the insecure type with a shriveled-up penis who hides behind ostentatious material things. So I can't possibly buy that phone.

Nokia phones run the gamut of offers. One tells me to "live life to the fullest and fulfill my active lifestyle." No thanks. That's what Gatorade is for. Another offers "irreplaceable luxury." Not for me: I drive a beat up Opel. One phone claims to be an "ideal training partner." I don't train; I drink beer. The last Nokia phone is billed as "practical meets merry." The last thing I want is a merry telephone. A phone should sit there and be quiet until I need it.

Motorola models start with the letter "V," which I think must stand for the English word Vain. One model claims to help me "strike a pose" and "turn heads." Another says it will "blast my senses." Great, a phone that's going to blast me.

Sony Ericsson has a device they say is both a Walkman and a camera (and presumably a telephone, too). It looks like it can do most everything for you, so I'm going to call Matis and alert him to it. He might want to get one for himself.

As for me, I think I'm going to stick with my blue telephone. The battery is dead now most of the time, but if something's important enough someone will surely come find me.

🄱🄰 That Long-gone Brezhnevian Charm

My first office was in the former Communist Party headquarters in Tartu, Estonia. It was 1992, and I was a Canadian volunteer, one of the new conquerors dispatched by my country to teach our way of life. I was given an office next to the county governor's, in part to give me some status, in part so he could keep his eye on me. My office had a padded door, a blaze orange sofa large enough to seat twelve comrades, a bookcase with the complete works of Vladimir Lenin, a large wooden abacus, and two telephones, one of them gray, the other red.

On the first day, I picked up the red phone to see if it might be a direct line to the Kremlin.

"Yes?" my secretary answered.

"Hello," I said, for lack of anything better.

"Yes?" she asked again.

"I would like a pizza," I said in my rudimentary Estonian.

"We have no pizza," she answered.

I got up and walked to the other side of the padded door. "That was a joke," I said. "I knew I couldn't get a pizza. I was just trying out the phone."

"Oh," she said, turning back to her nails. We had no computers, and so there wasn't email to hide behind. Doing one's nails in the office apparently wasn't a firing offense.

The second day in the office I was taken to a room full of plants, where a large, smiling woman removed her wedding ring and looped it through a length of ribbon. I was instructed to dangle the ring over each different kind of plant. Sometimes the ring spun clockwise, sometimes counterclockwise. Occasionally, it moved left to right. Sometimes right to left. In each case, the woman nodded, frowned, or grunted, making note of the movement.

"What am I doing here?" I finally asked, after she placed the wedding ring back on her finger.

"Some plants don't suit you," she explained. "I was finding out which."

Several days later, my office was a veritable garden, full of every sort of plant that my bioenergy wouldn't kill.

After six months in the office, I spoke enough Estonian to understand a little of what was going on. One of the governor's deputies was trading metal. When he wasn't trading metal, he was importing used cars from the USA or selling bulletproof jackets. He let me try on one of the jackets and took my photo.

There was a man on another floor who would call out to me in English whenever he saw me: "Horse thieves everywhere." I was never certain what he meant.

There was a café downstairs, and whenever the staff didn't feel like working, they placed a sign on the door which read *avarii*. This literally meant "accident," but the proprietress would always unlock the door and serve me a coffee and cognac.

I enjoyed that early Estonian office life. Every day was a new adventure. But as old men grieve everywhere, it ain't what it used to be.

Today, Estonian offices don't look any different than those I've seen in Finland. And compared to Canada, most Estonian offices are nicer.

For starters, the oldest technology in use is ten years old. Russian office equipment was worthless, so there was no choice but to buy modern western goods. And of course everyone here has the most modern mobile phone. The office furniture is all made in Scandinavia, or if it's locally made, it looks like it was made in Scandinavia.

There is still some frightening residue left over from the Soviet era. The elevator in our building is Soviet. It has no memory and can convey passengers to only one destination at a time. You don't ask "going up?" You get in and wait your turn for the button. My Finnish boss takes some comfort in the fact that an Otis sticker has been placed in the elevator. I haven't decided whether to tell him that Otis didn't make the elevator; they just service it. If he reads it here, I'll know why he's taking the stairs.

❷❶ Portrait of an Immigration Office

2007

'W'hat's this 'McCormick?'" asked the Estonian immigration official to whom I presented my residency permit application.

"It's my middle name," I replied.

"Why's it have a lower case 'C?'"

"I don't know. It's Irish. That's how it's written."

"But it's not that way on your passport. Your passport has an upper case 'C.'"

"I didn't realize that."

"Look!"

"You're right. On my passport it's written with an upper case 'C.'"

"Why?"

"All of the letters on my passport are written in upper case."

"Why?"

"I don't know. Do you want me to call the Canadian Embassy and ask? Is it that important to you?"

The official frowned.

2005

"Where'd you get that chair?" the official asked.

"From the desk next to you," I answered. There had been no chairs at her desk, and I wanted to sit.

"What if someone needs it?"

"No one needed it. I asked."

"Oh, you asked, did you?"

"I didn't steal it, if that's what you're suggesting."

"You should not take chairs from there. Someone might need them."

"Okay, from where would you like me to take a chair?"

"I said he could take the chair," interrupted the official's colleague at the next desk. "No one was using it."

"You take chairs from the big table," my official shouted. "Not from smaller tables!"

I returned the chair to my official's colleague's table and selected one from the large table behind me.

"There," I said. "I now have the correct chair. Shall we proceed?"

The official frowned.

1998

Until recently, residency permit applicants were required to provide the following: an original university diploma, certification by a state psychologist that they were not insane, and a certificate from a state clinic proving they were HIV negative.

"Do you have the additional documents required?" the official asked.

"I do." I presented him an envelope.

"I see here that you're HIV negative."

"Yes, I went to the state clinic and they administered the test."

"But how do I know you don't have AIDS?"

"I don't understand."

"The Estonian state needs to be certain you do not have AIDS. How do we know you don't have AIDS?"

"Because I'm HIV negative," I offered, still not sure what the man wanted.

"Yes, but how do I know you don't have AIDS?"

"If I'm HIV negative, then I don't have AIDS. Scientists tell us that to contract AIDS you must first have the HIV virus."

"Well, I'm not a scientist."

❷❶ My Customer, My Enemy

I n 1992, when I went to the state department store to purchase a winter hat, a gulf of two meters separated me from the rabbit-fur *shapka* I needed to keep warm. These two meters were patrolled by a grandmotherly figure who, when she deemed me worthy, removed the hat from the shelf and let me try it on. Once I found one that fit, I had to move to another line to pay, then return to the original line, wait my turn again, and present my receipt. The woman scrutinized the receipt, a tissue-thin paper which she then stacked neatly with others. Then she slowly wrapped my hat in white packing paper and tied it up with brown twine. The grandmotherly type was not known as a salesman, though she did, in a way, sell. In fact, except for her age, she wasn't much like a grandmother at all. She was invariably mean: As a customer, I was the enemy.

Back in those days there wasn't such a thing as sales. When the phone rang in the office where I worked, the secretary would lift the receiver a centimeter above its cradle and let it drop. She just couldn't be bothered. If she did decide to answer the phone, and if the desired party was out of the office, she would bark "Call back!" and abruptly hang up.

Sixteen years later, some things have changed.

We've got a great salesman at the magazine where I work. He's no different than an American salesman in the sense that he loves the thrill of the chase and the taste of the kill. When he sells an ad he dances around the office, pumping his arms like he's just scored a goal for Manchester United.

My regular squash partner was the top insurance salesman in Estonia. Sometimes, he walks and talks like a character from David Mamet's *Glengarry Glen Ross*. But my friend's commissions totaled more than his boss' salary, and so of course the boss fired him. He runs his own company now, where he doesn't have to worry about a boss.

But these two guys are mutants. For the most part, there are few real salesmen here. Most simply show up at their desk every day, put in a few phone calls, and get paid a measly salary. But I shouldn't complain. Rome wasn't built in sixteen years.

A British friend of mine owns a restaurant where Estonian diners have screamed at his waitresses for approaching their table uninvited. My friend's an emotional type, and he lets the customers know they're not welcome to just sit around and chat. They can do that at home, he tells them.

I visited the Mercedes dealership several weeks ago, spent twenty minutes ogling some pretty expensive cars. Four salesmen sat at their desks, and not one bothered to ask if I might not like to drive off in that 100,000-dollar roadster on the showroom floor. A couple of times I tried to make eye contact with the salesmen, but they looked away, as if they'd been caught stealing toilet paper rolls from the company bathroom.

If you visit the state department store today, you can touch the products, even try them on without assistance. Clerks patrol the floors and are glad to help — if you ask. It's said Estonians have an attitude that "service is servile." They've told me countless times that it's not in their character to serve. I think they're proud of it. But you can't eat pride, as my mother likes to say. And a lot of Estonians will eventually figure that one out.

But even today, when you call an office, it's rare to hear the words *May I take a message?* More often, you're told to call back, though usually you're told politely.

❷❷ Watching the Neighbor's House Burn

I didn't start to worry until the roof caught fire. When the asbestos shingles went, it sounded like a drive-by shooting.

Before that I thought the drunks were out in their yard burning leaves. So what if a burn ban had been in place for two weeks? Most Estonians pay no more attention to burn bans than they do traffic regulations.

But it wasn't the drunks' house. It was the mother and daughter's house next to the drunks. I seriously considered calling the fire department, but I ran to check it out first. Maybe the mother and daughter were tossing aerosol cans on the fire for fun? I'm perhaps sometimes too uptight, and what I consider an out-of-control fire doesn't at all coincide with the local definition. In the neighborhood I live, people generally shut up and mind their own business.

The brothel behind my house plays loud Russian rock and roll and the girls cackle like chickens throughout the summer, and no one complains. Children on mopeds run pedestrians off the streets, and no one complains. Dogs fill the park with excrement: no one cleans up, and no one complains. So I try to do the neighborly thing: I don't complain.

By the time I got to the house fire, a good crowd had gathered to watch. And the fire department was on the job. (Another Estonian peculiarity: Estonians like quiet; police and fire vehicles rarely use sirens.) The firemen unrolled their hoses and drenched the woodshed next to the mother and daughter's house. Of course, I don't know if they're mother and daughter; I just suspect. You see, I've never met them. In fact, after two years in the same house, I've only met one of my neighbors.

To gauge whether my time in Estonia has made me unfriendly, I asked my landlord if he knew any of the neighbors. He said he knows the same one I do. Estonians are true to the etymological meaning of neighbor: someone who lives nearby. But Estonian neighbors don't necessarily know each other. And, despite the urgings of Matthew 19:19, they don't necessarily love each other.

By never introducing myself to any of my neighbors, I was just trying to fit in. I was trying to do things the Estonian way.

So why do I feel so rotten about that house?

❷❸ Battle Stations

I've always loved Russia, if only for the Russians. They're a people to whom "*pazhalusta*" (please) and "*spasiba*" (thank you) actually matter, and even poorly spoken Russian will get you almost everything and everywhere. And there are few things better in life than to be the honored guest of a Russian. The host opens his heart and soul and "what's mine is yours" is more than a cliché.

Although I've been to Russia many times, I took my first trip to Moscow just last week. My prior love for Russia had come from the countryside: aimless wanderings in search of the people under Chekhov's mansard roof, Turgenev's sportsmen, or Pushkin's fog on the hills of Georgia.

But Moscow made me an urban fan. When I stepped into Red Square I could understand that Russia is a great nation in the word's true meaning and that the source of Russian pride is not misplaced. Young Muscovites were as stylish as New Yorkers and there was palpable energy on the streets. After a few days spoiled by my Moscow hosts, even the dirty metro seemed romantic and I began to find pleasant meter and rhyme in the exit signs: *V hod v gorod.*

But while individual Russians are a delight, a large group of them is entirely another matter. Courtesy of a cancelled Estonian Air flight — technical trouble, what's new? — I was to witness the dark underbelly of the Russian soul. Over the next nine hours — the time it would take Estonian Air's crack representatives to get us off the plane and re-ticketed for other destinations — I would be treated to an up-close tour of the uniquely Russian phenomenon of the line, or *ochered*.

Russian lines take on distinct forms that are not, in fact, lines. They are more elliptical in shape with cells within the larger unit each playing out its own small drama. It is much like being in the showroom of an electronics dealer with each television tuned to a different Mexican soap opera. Within cells of two or three persons, elbows are thrown, luggage carts driven over toes, and the raw cruelty of Darwinism is on full display.

It began on my flanks. I would turn my attention only briefly to the magazine I was reading, and dark shapes would appear in my peripheral vision. Wordlessly, they would infiltrate the queue and plant themselves directly before me.

From my days in Kiev, I thought I was sufficiently versed in the Russian line lingo — stern utterances such as *"zdyess ochered!"* (It's a line!) and *"ja stayu zdyess tozhe!"* (I'm standing here, too) — but my Ukraine experience proved not up to the major leagues of Moscow. Muscovites simply ignored me. When I employed eye contact, the western technique of shaming, Russians displayed total indifference. To them they'd achieved their new, rightful place in line, and any prior aggressiveness was now water under the bridge. A few smiled when I made eye contact. Most ignored me and went back to loud conversations with their friends.

I don't mind a little bit of lawlessness, and I have to admit fascination (and a bit of admiration) for the strange ways Russians behave. Many even cut to the very front of the line without the slightest protest from any other passenger, and I was spellbound by the silent charisma of those able to manage that feat. But when you are standing in line for nine hours, Russian behavior takes on a different significance. I realized I might never get out of Sheremetyevo Airport alive.

Despite my attempts to step up my level of aggressiveness there were always more people in front of me than behind. Something was amiss. I soon found myself at the very end of the line. How had that happened?

At the end of the queue I found other westerners. There was a middle-aged Italian businessman with no idea which line he was in. There was an elderly French couple who wanted to go to Prague. And there were a half-dozen Estonians who silently, patiently looked on. One of them acknowledged me when I rolled my eyes. "Are we ever going to get checked in?" I asked.

"It's a Russian thing," he shrugged. "I'm used to it." It's said Estonians are the ideal intermediaries for doing business in Russia. They're western enough to win Europe's trust, but their Soviet past enables them to smartly navigate the Russian system.

To the untrained eye it might have appeared the Estonians were standing idly by. But they had a plan. As I chatted with the man, I noticed the line was actually growing behind the Estonians. The Estonians did not push, shove, or swear. They had quietly formed a phalanx. In absence of spears and pikes, they employed luggage trolleys and heavy baggage to defend their flanks and gain forward ground. In characteristic Estonian style they did not invite me to join their phalanx, though they seemed not to object to my presence. And so I remained. In another two hours I had my ticket.

If any of my fellow passengers are reading this, I'd like to convey my sincere appreciation. You may not know it, but you saved my life. Had it not been for your assistance, I might be still queued up Sheremetyevo waiting on a sign from God. But, as it happened, you got me home and added a new chapter to my Russian education.

I'm scheduled to visit Moscow again next month. When the plane breaks down again, I can only pray you'll be there. I'll look for you in the queue and be ready to man my battle station.

❷❹ Suckers

O n a flight to New York, my wife Liina and I killed time reading the Skymall catalog. The Skymall is most wonderfully American: Even in a time of crisis, it sells what absolutely no one needs at prices almost everyone can afford. Such as:

Gravity Defyer Shoes which "propel you forward" ($129.95).

The Indoor Dog Restroom ($64.95).

The Marshmallow Shooter ($24.95, but $49.95 gets you one which shoots twice as far — 40 feet).

The Digital Camera Swim Mask ($99.95).

The Ultrasonic Eyeglasses Cleaner ($69.95).

The Germ-eliminating Knife Block ($89.95).

The Instant Doorway Puppet Theatre ($69.95).

The Animatronic Singing & Talking Elvis ($199.95).

Americans are so used to products like these that they don't find them unusual. It's said the average North American is bombarded by over five thousand advertising brand messages each day, so you might think we'd grow immune to Skymallesque stupidity.

Not my family.

A few years ago my mother gave me a Big Mouth Billy Bass, which is a battery-powered, rubber trophy fish mounted on a wooden plaque. It has a motion sensor, and when someone walks by, the fish thrashes about and sings a Bobby McFerrin tune ($19.99). The first time you see it you find it cute and clever. After the third time, you want to smash it to pieces with a baseball bat.

Liina likes to laugh at North America's out-of-control consumer culture, and she used to frequently remark about how gullible we are. She argued that Estonians were immune to such appeals. But later she had to eat her words.

When we lived in the United States, the first thing she fell for was the "12 CDs for a penny" mail-order offer: Get 12 for one cent in exchange for buying ten more over the next two years at "regular club prices." Liina pored over the catalog, selected the work of twelve artists, and taped her penny inside the envelope. Six weeks later the CDs arrived — along with a bill for 25 dollars for "shipping and handling." When she cancelled her membership she was obligated to return the CDs, and the return postage amounted to around three dollars. That's a hell of a lot of handling.

Lately, I've noticed that America's aggressive sales culture has gained ground in Estonia. The movement began quietly on the language front: before I knew it, Estonia had the verb *shoppama*, to shop. Soon after came Amway and a sales force trained in the invasion of private homes.

A company called Lux has been making the rounds selling vacuum cleaners, and their fast-talking sales rep left Liina no room to refuse what would turn out to be a one-and-a-half-hour long in-home sales pitch. But Liina, hardened in the USA, had a secret agenda to get our filthy couch cleaned for free.

I found a convenient excuse to be absent during the demonstration so that my credit card and bank information would be safe. Given how skeptical Estonians claim to be, I feared Estonian door-to-door salesmen would possess powers far beyond their western counterparts. I imagined the Lux rep as a middle-aged, thick-boned woman, a Guantanamo-trained, jackboot-wearing, Olivier-as-evil-dentist type who smiled but was at all times ready to deliver an electrical charge to your gonads in the name of clean floors. (She was probably an attractive twenty-something, but you can't be too careful.)

"Well, did you buy it?" I asked Liina when I returned home that evening.

"I don't have any money," she said. "But someday I'm going to buy it." After conning the sales rep into cleaning our sofa and two rugs, Liina was wowed by the product and its magical vibrasuck technology.

I tried to argue that it was cheaper to rent such a vacuum, or even hire a professional cleaner, than it was to pay two-thousand dollars, but Liina wasn't having any of it. She had concluded it was a superior product which could clean faster better. And maybe it could. I had to admit she does most of our vacuuming.

Friends tell me the Lux company is doing quite well in Estonia, especially selling to pensioners who don't have experience chasing away hard-driving salesmen. I'm told some buy two vacuums (one as a gift for the kids) and pay for them with leasing contracts. I don't know what business Estonian pensioners have buying a vacuum that expensive, but who am I to tell them what to do? I've still got Big Mouth Billy Bass on my wall.

In recent years, the same company who makes Billy Bass has developed a deer — named Buck, of course — a life-sized wiggling deer head which sings "Sweet Home Alabama," "Low Rider," and then farts loudly at the end of its performance ($150). Every time I visit my mother, I pray that she hasn't seen it in stores.

②⑤ A Pocket Guide to Expats

'W hy are you here?" is the question every local wants to put to foreigners. We have our stock answers, and often they're true. Sometimes, though, the foreigner leaves out part of the story. He doesn't want to admit he was fired from his job in Canada, or that he was caught on videotape robbing a Buenos Aires bank.

In American cowboy movies, if you weren't smart enough to know cattle rustlers were bad, the moviemakers put them in black hats. It happens to be the simplest way to categorize foreigners in the Baltic:

THE WHITE HATS

1. Smart but lazy. He would have been a success story anywhere but likes the fact he can earn good money in the region working comparatively little. He puts in a half day of real work and still outdoes the locals. (Everyone likes to talk about how hard working Baltic people are, but this is polite nonsense. As one Estonian put it, "The Germans taught us to work, and we did it very well. Then the Russians came and taught us not to work. And we learned that well, too.")

2. Regional Corporate Babysitter. He's a businessman dispatched to represent an international company. He is well educated, often smart, and will move on in three years. If he's single, he hangs out at Nimeta pub in the old city. If he's married, he spends his time trying to find activities for his wife.

3. The idle wife. Her husband is the regional corporate babysitter. He has a work permit, but she can't get one. Hers is not an easy life, especially if she's childless. She often does charity work or joins a book club to pass the time.

4. The female professional. These women are descendants of Sisyphus. (There used to be a good-news/bad-news joke about women's liberation in the Baltics: The bad news is that women's lib is coming; the good news is it won't be here for a hundred years.) There are few foreign female professionals here, and the reason is their lives are hard. In the workplace, the Baltic glass ceiling isn't glass; and in terms of a social life, most foreign women aren't interested in dating local men.

5. The Adventurer. He hates the nine-to-five grind of his previous western existence. He thrives here on the difficulties of daily life and the fact that there is still a surprise around every corner. He enjoys the fact that his friends at home view him as something of an oddball.

6. Married a local. These fall into two subcategories : (a) He who came here with the express purpose to find a woman — often a pensioner-divorcee from the USA, and (b) He who accidentally fell in love. Members of both groups generally feel like they've won the lottery.

7. Our Man in Havana. Nice work if you can get it. Who among us never wanted to be James Bond?

8. Foreign Estonians.

    i. Young exiles. Usually the twenty-something son of a genuine exile. He owns seven black turtlenecks and smokes cigarillos. He hasn't yet realized he's not on the set of Casablanca. Some say this type of foreign exile was "screwed twice by the former USSR: once after WWII, when he was given an exile identity, and again in 1991, when that identity was taken away."

    ii. True believers. He's a foreign Estonian/Latvian/Lithuanian who is truly committed to a better country. He's worked for the government since independence. And loved every minute of it.

    iii. Finally home. He's an older foreign Estonian/Latvian/Lithuanian who never quite fit in in his adopted country. He spoke with an accent and was made fun of. He never fully accepted life as a Canadian, American, or Australian. Now, he's finally returned home, where he again speaks with an accent and is made fun of.

THE BLACK HATS

1. The criminal. He's here doing what he's been disallowed in his home country. Perhaps he was banned from serving on boards of directors or banned from trading stock. He often moves in the highest circles of society or government. He is rarely caught, but when he is, it's quickly hushed up in the local press.

2. Talented Mr. Ripley. So you always wanted to be a brain surgeon? Don't let a little lack of education stop you. Fancy being the Duke of Edinburgh? Who's to say you're not? The Baltics are the perfect place to live dreams the home country wouldn't allow. Me, for example. Have you checked me out?

3. Unemployable back home. He is such an obvious idiot that no company back home will employ him longer than three months. In this region, he'll last a year.

4. Mr. Dysfunctional. He is mostly harmless, usually likeable, but has trouble getting out of bed in the morning. He tells people he's a writer but hasn't yet picked up the pen. He never pays for his own drinks, because he's always broke. He's held down jobs in the region, but never for very long.

5. The Mystery Man. No one is quite sure why he's here. And he himself isn't talking. At parties, he sits quietly in the background, sipping whisky and listening to others. You suspect Interpol might be interested in him, but he hasn't been anything but nice to you.

❷❻ I'm from the government and I'm here to help you.

'I'm from the government and I'm here to help you" is one of three punch lines to an American dirty joke. The line is prompted by the question, "What are the three biggest lies in the world?" I can't tell you the other two, because my column might be banned from print media.

In government's effort to help, it seems there are few things left to ban.

In order to combat child obesity, junk food ads were banned on television during certain hours in the UK. Food advertising is already banned during certain times, and toy advertising may soon follow.

In the USA, ads for three weight loss products — Exercise in a Bottle, Fat Trapper, and Fat Trapper Plus — were, in recent years, banned.

In Scotland, lap-dancing clubs are banned from advertising near schools.

In the UK, television stars may soon be banned from advertising liquor.

A bit closer to home, Russia recently banned beer advertising.

In Lancashire, UK, car owners may soon be banned from putting "For Sale" signs in windows of their cars.

Elsewhere in the UK, a businesswoman was banned from advertising for "hard-working" staff. It was ruled that the adjective discriminated against those who aren't hardworking.

I realize some of the bans were well-intended. In fact, thanks to no more Exercise in a Bottle, it's possible Americans are living healthy lives. But I'm skeptical. I'm also skeptical about Russia's ban on beer advertising, since every kiosk in every Russian city stocks beer, is open 24-7, and requires no minimum age for purchase. But what do I know? I just work here.

Every ad to air on one of the big three networks in the USA must be pre-approved by network censors. As a young ad man, it was my job to get network approval for ads from one of Japan's biggest electronics companies. We advertised video games, and the networks wanted to make sure we weren't putting impure thoughts into the heads of American children.

One of the games was called Splatterhouse. The object was to enter a slaughter-house with an axe and slice the artery of anything that got in your way. If you killed enough and got tired of the axe, you could upgrade to a chainsaw. At the end of the commercial red blood flowed from the top of a black screen to spell the word Splatterhouse. The censors approved that one and many others like it.

The network censors often denied approval on first review, but you could usually persuade them to see things your way. After all, they couldn't ban everything or there'd be no revenue. As long as we weren't showing fully-exposed female breasts, or using the F-word, then the censors would let it pass after a short conversation. Like human beings everywhere, they just wanted to be listened to.

Most recently at an English-language magazine to which I contribute, they've been wrestling with the issue of whether to accept ads for striptease clubs. Like all magazine publishers, they like ad revenue, and the strip clubs in the Baltic are more than ready to advertise.

On one hand, the services they offer are legal, and some of our readers undoubtedly visit the clubs. On the other hand, some of our readers find strip clubs appalling. And while striptease may or may not be appalling, some of the ads certainly are. Some scale new heights in bad taste, offering a two-dimensional lap-dance right on the page.

One of our competitors decided to accept the ads several years ago. The publisher was deluged with mail from wives of expatriate businessmen. "Remove the ads or my husband's company will no longer advertise with you" was a common letter. One woman wrote with the threat to "cancel my free subscription."

I don't know what we'll decide about striptease ads in our magazine. But I am glad we get to make the decision without government interference. The Baltic governments are rightly more worried about kids carrying handguns and shooting their classmates than they're worried about kids seeing a breast. And lucky for us, Smith & Wesson hasn't yet asked to advertise.

②⑦ Toilet Tour

This past summer, one of the tour companies in Tallinn allowed me the pleasure of guiding American cruise passengers. The company knew I hadn't passed any of the guide exams, but they still gave me the job. On my first day of work I realized why.

"Where's the bathroom?" two American women cried in unison. The bus had just cleared the cruise pier and we weren't two minutes into our tour. The women were close to seventy and had undoubtedly raised kids who'd pestered them with the same question. So I gave them the parental answer: "Didn't you go before you left the boat?" They had. But they needed to go again.

"Is everything here uphill?" another asked when we parked near the Tall Hermann tower and slogged up Toompea hill. "I don't like uphill." Some were grossly overweight and I found it hard to believe they'd read the brochure which makes it abundantly clear they'd have to walk several kilometers over uneven surfaces and climb a number of steps.

On Toompea, a bunch of them disappeared into a bathroom and suddenly my group had shrunk. The tour company doesn't have a lot of rules, but a couple of them are cardinal: Keep the group happy, and return to the boat with the same number of tourists you started with.

"Why are we standing around?" a man demanded. I told him I wasn't allowed to leave anyone behind. We would have to wait for them to return from the toilet.

"But that's not fair to the rest of us!"

I admitted he was right.

"Hey," a woman squared up to me in front of the group. "You have to tell us what to do. Order us around."

"How old are you?" I asked.

"Sixty-eight," she replied.

"I'm forty-three," I said. "I'm not old enough to be your mother." She dropped her hands from her hips. I had scored a direct hit. I turned from her and informed the group that I was here to talk about Estonia's fascinating history, and if they wanted to listen they were welcome. But if they wanted to spend their time touring Tallinn's toilets, I wasn't going to wrestle them to prevent it. "If you want to leave, you can easily find your boat. Walk to the sea and look for the biggest object in the water."

During the lunch break, I talked to a veteran Estonian guide who told me many guides won't work with Americans because they behave like children. "I know it's not easy," he said. "But you really do have to boss them around. It's what they want."

After lunch, I took the guide's advice and things improved. My new take-no-shit attitude worked wonders. The Americans filed right in, listened carefully, and a few even won my genuine respect by posing intelligent questions. I think they appreciated me for moving things along, but also for not trying to pretend that the Olympic Sailing Center is one of the Seven Wonders of the World. Instead, I pointed to the TOP Hotel and quoted P.J. O'Rourke on Soviet construction ("Commies love concrete, they just don't know the recipe"). I told the story of how the clever Estonians used the Olympics to get Moscow's money to fix up the Old Town. I explained the situation with Estonian pensions as we stood before Nevsky Cathedral's begging babushkas (the tourists gave them coins), and I didn't try to deny that most souvenirs are crap ("You're right, Mrs. Finkelstein. Your granddaughter could make a better painting of St. Nicholas Church"). In the Old Town square, where you couldn't beat the juxtaposition, I described the Soviet housing blocks of Lasnamäe and why someone would have preferred to give up a regal home in the Old Town in exchange for a two-room flat with hot water and a flush toilet.

But despite my perceived success (the Americans tipped me well), I didn't have the job long. Perhaps word got back to headquarters that I wasn't telling the right stories. Perhaps I wasn't subservient enough. But I thought the group appreciated it when I handed a woman an empty Coke bottle after she demanded the entire group return to the ship just so she could pee in a friendly toilet.

In the end, I didn't mind losing the job. I'm not cut out for guiding. A good guide combines the patience of a kindergarten teacher with the discipline of a drill sergeant. He can stick to the program but deftly deflect questions about Estonia's AIDS- or suicide-rate from an astonishingly well-read tourist. For better or worse, I don't fit that description. Even my mother once told me I wasn't cut out for diplomacy: *One day, buster, your mouth is going to get you in a lot of trouble.*

But I'm glad I tried the job. I acquired new skills. I'm now able to force-march forty American octogenarians up a hill they don't want to climb. I mastered a tone of voice that makes a battalion snap to attention. And I learned Tallinn geography as only the elite few know it: I can tell you the precise longitude and latitude of every public and private toilet in the Old Town. And who wouldn't find that knowledge useful?

❷❽ Under a Bridge with Mr. Ansip

T here's a tasteless tax joke circulating among expat businessmen:
*How do you recognize Estonian businessmen abroad? They're the
ones who've brought their own sandwiches.*

I've been traveling lately and doing my best to live within the bounds set by the Estonian government: about 40 dollars per day and an average hotel cost of 170 dollars per night. If you travel to major cities that's not an easy task. To live on that amount often requires a night or two in youth hostels or sleeping under a bridge and looking for your food in dumpsters. I've often wondered how Estonian politicians do it. I've never seen a parliamentarian under my bridge.

Despite Estonia's flat tax and zero levy on corporate earnings, the rest of the program isn't so hot. I sometimes feel as if government is trying to confine Estonian business to the minor leagues. World-class companies understand two things: they need to keep their employees both healthy and smart. Sick employees raise your expenses, and stupid ones reduce your revenue. All first-rate companies provide programs to keep their employees exercising, eating right, and constantly learning something new. But try that in Estonia and the company is stuck with a 75 percent fringe benefits tax.

Mr. Ansip, as I understand, defends the program by saying the rules are clear and they work, and therefore no change is called for. I'll grant him the clear part, but I take issue with how well the system works.

I have a young Estonian friend (he's 25) who is terribly frustrated because he sees few prospects of getting rich. As a teen, he witnessed the boom years of the Estonian economy where a lot of people made piles of dough. My friend complains about the small size of the market, the fact that people think small — a litany of things most of which I find tedious. But I find something hopeful in the fact that he is an impatient, greedy, over-confident young man of the sort you encounter in every capitalist country. He isn't looking for a government handout and what little he remembers of the Soviet past comes through listening to his parents. You can say you don't like his priorities, but you have to admit he's normal, as far as ambitious, greedy, business-school types go.

The kid often asks me for advice (why I'm not sure; I'm not rich and unlikely to ever be) and I always tell him the same thing: The rich westerners I know didn't get that way by pursuing money; they were interested in something more, and they usually were passionate about something. I tell the kid he should decide what most lights his fire and throw himself at the feet of the best teacher he can find. "But then I'll have to leave Estonia," he says. He probably will. But if he really wants it, he shouldn't complain. That's how life is.

Sadly, though, I don't see the Estonian government doing a hell of a lot to keep smart kids hanging around. At the most basic level, the government makes doing business in major markets inconvenient and expensive. And they don't seem willing to lift a finger when private enterprise wants to do its part to keep the population both healthy and educated.

I'm sure there are ways around these rules, but I'm good at only a certain number of things and rule dodging isn't one of them. If Mr. Ansip truly worships the simplicity of the tax system, then he can surely empathize with someone who can't be bothered to look for loopholes just so he can find a way to eat three full meals every day and stay in a decent hotel in Moscow.

Things will eventually change. They simply have to. Estonia's frequent role model, Finland, has a system which seems perfectly normal. According to the Finnish tax office, expenses for an employee's job-related graduate education are a deductible business expense for Finnish companies. And with regard to travel, the per diem allowance for a Finn in Moscow is, for example, 100 dollars. (A Finn in Estonia, by the way, is allowed 64 dollars per diem.) Hotel compensation for a Finn abroad is, not surprisingly, limited to the "amount shown on a receipt."

The good news is that in every country most silly legislation is eventually amended or repealed. But until then, until the day inevitable reason and good sense set in, I'm waiting for you, Mr. Ansip. I've saved you a warm, dry spot underneath my favorite bridge.

❷❾ How to Get Chicks

Experts tell us that advertising to women is as complicated as courting them. Say the wrong thing, you're dead as a beef.

Some American studies claim women account for 80 percent of all purchases, so we had better treat them right. Experts say women like bold, easy-to-read signs. They like good lighting and are appalled by burned-out bulbs in stores. They like soft background music. They like to imagine how products fit into the home — curvy digital cameras and flat-screen TVs were made because of women.

And what don't they like? They don't like reaching up too high to get something from the top shelf. They don't like crowded stores. Most of all, they don't like having their asses touched. I'm not talking about courting; I'm talking about cramped aisles. Marketers call it the "butt-brush factor." If your product is located in a narrow aisle packed with people, a woman may just pass you by.

Men, on the other hand, are simple. Recently, I was dazzled by an ad for the Estonian army. The ad showed all the cool toys a recruit can play with: a Mercedes G-wagon, a German submachine gun, night vision goggles. And you can wear camouflage every day of the week.

I have to say this appealed to me, and it made we want to join the Estonian army. But while I liked the ad, it didn't work with Estonians. "Not everyone aspires to be an assistant machine gunner," explained one military official. The British, who advise the Estonians on military matters, suggested targeting young men doing their obligatory service. Perhaps men who've already experienced the life, the Brits reasoned, might want to make it a career. So the Estonians stopped advertising. And I stopped yearning to join up.

Currently, the Estonian army is after women. "Have you ever thought what you could do to make your country better?" reads a page on the army website devoted to women. "How will you fulfill your obligations as a citizen?" I think the British may need to step in again, because it's obvious the Estonian army knows nothing about marketing to women. Talk about the soft lighting in the barracks. About the high thread count on military sheets. And the fact that butt-brushing never occurs in the military.

❸❶ When English Trumps Estonian

Once in line at Selver, a Russian speaker in front of me succeeded in both disarming and charming a hostile Estonian checker. Within seconds she was under his spell, her grumpiness gone. She was smiling, laughing, pleased at the prospects of life.

I'm told Russians have a saying that for every language you speak, you live another life. If that's true, then I was witness to the Russian man drawing the Estonian into his world, seeing her born again outside the prison of her Nordic silence.

When I moved to Estonia sixteen years ago, my bad Estonian got a very positive reaction. Salesgirls were happy to suffer patiently along as I inquired about sprats in oil versus sprats in mustard sauce. Estonian families were thrilled to serve me the kolkhoz's finest carp and listen intently as I butchered the case endings of their impossible language. (Only the telephone office people were mean to me, but I'm convinced they were born that way.) In most cases, the simple fact that I attempted Estonian was treated as the ultimate compliment to the new republic and its citizens.

Since my mother rarely spoke Estonian to me growing up, I did not arrive in Estonia fluent in the language. I spoke it so badly that, except for my Estonian name, no one ever mistook me for a foreign Estonian. My accent was so strange no one confused me for a Russian, either. Once, after struggling to order a cut of sausage from behind my local meat counter, as I walked away I heard one worker whisper to another: "That German boy is always so polite."

I worked hard to escape my German phase. I found excellent Estonian teachers and learned a good deal more sitting on a bar stool. But as my Estonian improved, I discovered the quality of service decreased in direct proportion. The better I spoke Estonian, the worse Estonians treated me.

When my "*tere*" (hello) no longer reeked of foreign origins, the "tere" was no longer appreciated. While in longer conversations my odd grammatical choices and slight accent would give me away, short, quotidian transactions did not betray me and I was no longer special. I had to push and shove like everyone else.

I missed being different. I missed hearing the common refrain: "*Te räägite eesti keelt nii hästi. Venelased on siin elanud viiskümmend aastat ja nemad ei oska ühtegi sõna*" ("You speak Estonian so well. The Russians have lived here fifty years and don't know a single word.") Neither of those was actually true — my Estonian wasn't so hot, and I knew plenty of Russians who could speak Estonian — but it was still always nice to hear.

Perhaps Estonian from the mouths of foreigners is no longer novel. I recently saw a television show where it seemed every Dutchman living in Tallinn spoke the Estonian language better than I. I even know some Americans who've learned it; a few of them actually speak it well.

As I watched the Russian man charm the Selver checker, I was jealous of his gift to change the world with language. Standing in the queue, I thought I should perhaps study a foreign language. But then I realized, I already speak one. English! To me, it hardly seems foreign, but it could indeed be a weapon with which to subdue a hostile service industry employee.

"Good afternoon!" I exclaimed to the checker, giving her my best American-style smile. She had just come off the high of the Russian experience, and now was getting a jolt of the optimism inherent in English-language small talk. "I brought my Partner Card!" I sang, thrusting it over the countertop before she could ask.

She was pleased to receive me and was all smiles. She replied "good afternoon" in serviceable English and was not angry at all when I wanted to add a plastic bag after she'd already rung up my other items. She was still smiling when she told me how much I owed: "Five hundred and sixty-two kroons." I'd never been so pleased to pay so much for groceries. "But may I have my free *Postimees*?" I asked. She shot me a strange look. Having spent over five hundred kroons I was indeed entitled to a free newspaper, but what would a foreigner want with *Postimees*? Her expression begged to know if I'd been putting her on? Could I have been making fun of her? Could I have taken her to such new emotional heights, only to drop her without a parachute?

"The newspaper," I recovered. "It's for my Estonian wife."

The checker exhaled, relieved. She smiled and handed me the paper. "Have a nice day," she said. And she meant it.

Since then, I've made English my service language. I speak English at the post office, in restaurants, with FedEx, and with Estonian airport security. Most are more than pleased to practice their English, and I get far better service than the Estonians before and after me in the queue.

It's a sad fact of life at the moment that English trumps Estonian. But I haven't given up on my Estonian. I still use it at home. I speak it with my wife, who is always happy to help me polish it and make it better than the day before. Someday, I know, an Estonian speaker will get equal or better service than an English speaker. And when that day comes, I'll be ready.

❸❶ Dress for Success

D ress for success in Estonia used to mean tracksuits. *Dressin-imesed* they were called. An Adidas three-stripe navy track-suit accessorized with a gold chain and shoebox-sized mo-bile phone were the height of fashion.

A prominent Tallinn lawyer I knew liked to mock the trend, saying tracksuits were worn only by uneducated Russian thugs and Estonian *kantpead*, or boxheads, as they were known. But I soon learned to treat that statement with the same regard as an American who says he doesn't like McDonald's (sooner or later you'll catch him eating there). One Sunday I rode my bicycle by the lawyer's house and there he was, out walking his dog in a bright red tracksuit.

Soon after the tracksuits came the black clothing phase. Men wore black t-shirts and black jeans. A boss of mine wore this outfit every day. He bathed daily — or at least he came to work with wet hair — but he only washed his outfit once a week. Sunday was the day he'd don his old tracksuit so his wife could launder the black stuff. Black may have hid dirt, but it didn't hide smell, so we all tried to schedule meetings with him for Mondays and Tuesdays. After that we communicated by phone.

Estonians are currently living in the sportswear phase. T-shirts with logos and brand names printed are worn not as casual wear, but in the workplace, as well. Even some of the nation's most credible television journalists wear branded-sportswear on the air, making them appear less like journalists and a lot more like MTV veejays.

Designer dresswear is also popular. In North America, most businessmen, even rich ones, don't dress head to toe in Armani or Hugo Boss, but there are plenty of them here that do. If it weren't for their pale Nordic faces, it would be hard to tell many Estonian businessmen from the drug lords and pimps in a Harlem police lineup.

Of course, most who participate in these trends aren't actually wealthy but are out to look wealthy. The real rich people I've known rarely even spend a few minutes to consider their wardrobes.

I used to work with one of the wealthiest men in America. He was oblivious to fashion. He often turned up at the office wearing white athletic socks with his Church's English shoes. He'd put on whatever was in his drawer without much regard, and I recall sitting across from him at a meeting where the black printed text on his t-shirt showed through his white pinpoint oxford: *Ask me about my grandkids.*

But I don't wish to sit in judgment of how Estonian businessmen dress for success. Just because it amuses me doesn't mean I'm above falling victim to it. While I never bought the tracksuit (I was tempted), I did buy the black jeans. They seemed immensely practical. Black goes with any other color (including black), and the color doesn't require thought. So on a trip home to Toronto I bought a pair. I got the same relaxed-fit Levis I always wore but in high-fashion black. I proudly wore them to the office, and stood by my boss for a photograph.

When the photo was printed I understood why only trendy people should follow trends. I was and would always be a sartorial loser. My boss' jeans were the tight-fitting Armanis and mine were cowboy jeans. Next to a svelte, athletic Estonian young businessman, I was a pudgy, middle-aged Canadian who was trying to look cool. The relaxed-fit jeans made it even worse — they sagged in the back like a little boy had made a turd in them.

But I'm not the only one. Plenty of foreigners here get sucked into fashion. Recently, I attended a barbecue where a visiting American friend was prompted to ask about other Americans at the party: "Who are all these dandies?" There was a 45-year-old who wore black patent leather shoes and covered his potbelly with a pink polo shirt He declared everything "phat" and refused take off his sunglasses indoors. Another guy wore pinstripes, an electric pink shirt, and had a greased-down Caesar haircut. "Uh, they just came from work," I explained. "Working as what?" he demanded. "Undercover vice?"

I've started to look for solace in the truly rich. Luckily, some rich Estonians are just as pleasantly oblivious as my wealthy American colleague.

I know one super rich Estonian guy who lives in a tiny, ground-floor apartment with a view of the parking lot. I looked in his cupboard and discovered a random collection of dishes: two plates, one bowl, and three forks. He doesn't own a car, because he doesn't know how to drive. I've only ever seen him wear one pair of shoes, and half the time he wears shorts hiked up under his armpits. Even in winter. He likes the simple pleasures in life like bicycle riding and playing his stereo too loud. I've told him repeatedly that if he'd allow Estonia's sleazy tabloid, *Kroonika*, to profile him, he'd be doing a service to the rest of us. What a breath of fresh air it would be for the nation to meet a wealthy Estonian who's never owned a tracksuit, black jeans, or the latest from Versace. And if we all started wearing short pants hiked up near our armpits, it wouldn't be an awful thing. Or at least no worse than our tracksuit days.

❸❷ The Word I Fear

When I'm out of beer money and the kids haven't eaten in a while, I write for English-language magazines in the region, often doing reviews of hotels. Last week, I received a letter from an Estonian hotel marketing manager who told me that if I didn't change a sentence in the review of his hotel, our "good cooperation could no longer be possible." What cooperation was that, I wondered? I'd never met the guy, never spoken to him, never even heard of him.

Of course, "cooperation" in Estonian means "might give you money," meaning he was threatening to possibly never advertise in the future. Never mind that he'd never advertised in the past. Ever.

What's more important, he couldn't grasp the idea that editorial could be independent from advertising. The market is rife with "cooperation": Many Estonian journalists don't pay for meals in restaurants they review, nor do they pay for treatments in the spas they write about. In fact, there's only one Estonian daily that forbids "sponsorship" of its travel and automotive writers. It's that sort of cooperation.

"Cooperation" in the Estonian vernacular has long departed from its dictionary definition: common benefit. Estonian marketing managers somehow never saw the dictionary; they only saw the Hollywood movies where the bad guy takes a hostage: *If you cooperate, nobody gets hurt.* In the marketing manager's worldview, he has a gun to my head. If I shut up and write what he tells me, he just might consider advertising. He sees himself as so powerful that he doesn't have to let his hostage go — he only has to think about letting him go.

Cooperation is the most abused word in Estonian business, and I invite you, dear reader, to purge it from your vocabulary. And next time someone suggests you cooperate, reply that you too have seen the movie, and the bad guy never lets the hostage go.

By the way, the English-language magazine was a reputable one, and they solved the problem by removing the hotel's listing. If a hotel treats a journalist like that, can you expect them to treat a guest any better? And, besides, there are still plenty of other hotels in Estonia. Places you can stay without fear of cooperation.

❸❸ Heroes

An American friend of mine recently got shot. Paul was having a beer on his front porch and two thugs showed up to rob his neighbor as she was parking her car. He began shouting and so they shot him in the neck. After Paul was released from the hospital he had to hide out at hotels and friends' homes for two weeks, which is how long it took the media to quit staking out his house.

Now the media says he's a hero. I called to tell my dad, who also knows Paul, and he remarked, "Geez, what an unfortunate son of a bitch." Hero or unfortunate son of a bitch? In America, it's a fine line that separates them.

Americans have a lot of heroes. In addition to Paul, they've got Superman, Batman, Spider-Man, Catwoman, the Incredible Hulk, and the Green Lantern. Heroes in America — or superheroes, as the case may be — are more than just guys in silly costumes; they're manifestations of the belief that Team America can right the wrongs of the world and that there is still hope for the world's huddled masses and wretched refuse. Not a bad sentiment, actually.

I have to admit I miss superheroes, and I wish Estonia had a few. Even one would do, and he doesn't need to fly. I'd send him out on missions to foster simple kindness. He'd inspire men to hold doors for ladies (and the ladies to say thank you). He'd champion all that stuff President Ilves says about wanting Estonians to be more supportive of one another. And if I'm allowed to give my hero super-strength, I'd have him overturn the cars of arrogant drivers who park wherever they please, starting with that blue Ferrari which I often see on the Radisson's sidewalk.

I'd send him over to Estonian Air to have a conversation with the claims rep who told me my flight was cancelled due to a "flight safety problem in the Moscow airport," instead of admitting, as Moscow's ground supervisor confirmed, that it was a malfunction of the plane's air pressure receiver gauge.

My Estonian superhero would shake up the builder who took my money, disappeared for sixty days, and then reappeared claiming his chronic alcoholism was a "virus."

And I'd send him downstairs to counsel my wife's nutty aunt, who chases social workers away by screaming at them because they bought the wrong potatoes, the wrong cabbage, or the cherries which she believed were too sour.

Later on, once he's tackled the simple things, I'd give him the power of flight and send him down to Georgia to do and say the things which are too frightening a job for the superheroes from the superpower. Then, having wrapped that up, he could fly back home and have a word or two with Tallinn's Mayor Edgar Savisaar.

Perhaps a superhero is too much for Estonia. However, the ideas represented by heroes aren't out of reach. Estonian journalists seek them, scouring the earth for heroes with the tiniest percentage of Estonian blood. An editor once asked me to profile an American businessman with an Estonian grandmother. "But why him?" I asked. He didn't seem special to me — just another garden-variety rich dude. "Because," the editor replied, "we have so few good role models in our own country."

It may be un-Estonian to seek the spotlight and take credit for good deeds, but any nation capable of Good Service Month can surely create a modest superhero, or at least promote the common man who does uncommon things. There's no need to get carried away like the Americans who find heroes under every rock. "They're all heroes," President Bush once said about the victims of 9-11. But Mr. Bush has never owned a dictionary. Most were simply people who were in the wrong place at the wrong time. Like my friend Paul, the unfortunate son of a bitch.

I've argued about this topic with my wife, Liina, and she says Estonians don't have the same worries as Americans and therefore don't need heroes. Liina says only nations with superproblems require superheroes. She may have a point. While Estonia may not have superheroes, you're also not likely to get shot in the neck while sitting on your own front porch.

❸❹ My Archaeological Dig

As carefully as a scholar unearthing an Egyptian tomb, I dug into the ground of my garden. Every spade of overturned soil produced a Soviet artifact: a vinegar bottle, a rusted tin of sprats, an empty vodka bottle. Most commonly, I found the vodka bottle. And so, as any good scientist would do, I formulated my null hypothesis: Soviet citizens were extremely fond of drink. And I continued to dig.

I considered revising my null hypothesis. Should it be Soviet gardeners were fond of drink? Because why else would one find so many empty vodka bottles in a three-square meter plot of earth where rhubarb was most recently grown? But I kept my hypothesis general, because the gardeners I have known from the Soviet Union were sober nature lovers, and because an impromptu dig at my sister-in-law's summer house produced similar results — the place had been the summer residence for tractor mechanics from a kolkhoz. Soviet mechanics, as laws of the universe dictate, love their vodka. And so I kept my null hypothesis general, since you never know when a bunch of tractor mechanics might show up and want to hang around your garden.

Sadly, the bottles just kept coming. True, intermittently I found a plastic lid for a jar used for canning vegetables (or moonshine). I found a few bottle caps which might have been from soda (or beer). But the evidence mounted at such a rate that I, as a man of science, could not ignore it. I could not dismiss my null hypothesis. I know that's not nice to say. And I truly hope I get a lot of mail from other scientific-minded readers who can poke holes in my methodology and produce irrefutable scientific evidence that the Soviets who buried the crap in my garden were not single-mindedly devoted to drinking.

Why was I digging the garden up in the first place? you ask. Because my wife ordered a truckload of soil which turned out to be compost. She was attempting to plant some variety of evergreen, so I was ordered to dig up the good soil out of the garden (where would be planted things which do not hate compost) in order to place the garden soil around the evergreens, which were, by the way, to block the neighbors' view of our driveway. Complicated, I know. I was just following orders.

Despite the depression that set in about Soviet citizens, each unearthed ancient empty vodka bottle began to produce thirst. After the twelfth bottle, I could stand it no more. I put down my spade and marched directly to my freezer, where I always have one 750 ml bottle of Saaremaa Viin, the absolute best Estonian vodka money can buy. I filled a silver cup and raised my glass to Soviet citizens, gardeners, and even tractor mechanics. As I threw back my third shot, I formed another null hypothesis: American gardeners are extremely fond of drink. And I raised my glass again. All in the name of science.

❸❺ Shrooming

'**H**ey, I'm out mushrooming!" an American friend phoned to tell me. There was joy in his voice. He was a city boy who rarely experienced nature.

"Alone?"

"No. With some Estonians."

"So they tell you which ones to pick?"

"No. I just pick the ones that look nice."

"How do you know which ones are poison?"

"Oh, I don't eat them."

"So you let the Estonians eat the poisonous ones?"

"Oh, come on," he sighed. "I think the people who eat them will know the difference!"

And so it goes with most foreigners picking mushrooms in Estonia. We wander through the forest wondering whether that man on horseback might be a milkcap. In the end, not wanting to suffer the shame of returning empty handed, we give up and put both in our sack. You could say we adopt the wartime cry of the infantryman: *Shoot 'em all. Let God sort 'em out.*

I've mushroomed for over ten years now with Estonians from Valga in the south to Tallinn in the north, and I'm still as confused as the day I started. The only mushroom I can identify for sure is the chanterelle. I like it not only because it's tasty and easy to indentify, but because when I bring a basketful to an Estonian family I don't have to hear "Oh, thanks, but these are *ussitanud*." As I've been led to believe, the chanterelle is the only mushroom the worms won't eat.

I've guest-mushroomed with dozens of Estonian families, and no two experiences have been alike.

"We only pick porcini," a grandmother told me. "We leave the others to rot."

"But what about this one?" I asked, proudly displaying one I thought looked edible.

"Elk's mouth," she replied. "Slightly poisonous. Leave it for the Russians."

On another trip with a Hiiumaa family, the father explained we'd be picking only gypsy mushrooms and sheathed woodtufts. I had a tough time finding them and would occasionally run to him with one I'd picked with a previous family. He'd shrug his shoulders as if to say, *Well, if you insist.*

After my third or fourth mushrooming trip, I concluded that every Estonian is a mushroom snob of a different kind. And there's no predicting which kind. If there is any pattern to the snobbery, it's that Estonians will often leave something called *tatikad.* I'm still not sure which ones they are, except that they're slimy, and I generally try to avoid slimy things.

My basic mushrooming education was given me by a woman with the last name of Kuus, which means "six" in Estonian. She was a tough, charismatic woman from Southern Estonia, who her friends called "*poolseitse,*" or six-and-a-half, because, due to her strong personality, they felt she was just a little bit more than six. She loaned me a pair of old rubber boots, put a basket and knife in my hands, and set out to teach me the tricks of the trade. "You're walking right past them!" was her refrain of the day. Poolseitse was well into her sixties, wore thick coke-bottle glasses when she read, but she could spot a false morel at fifty meters without any optical aid. Despite my ignorance, she saw something in my soul and refused to give up on me. She made a hell of an effort to educate me, and I'm sorry to report I let her down. I never became a mushroom *meister.*

Many of my expatriate friends have asked if I could bring them hallucinogenic mushrooms. I'm not quite sure which ones they are, though a friend once pointed them out to me: bright red with white spots. I believe they're called fly agaric. But there are both big ones and small ones which match the description, and the friend who pointed them out was an ornithologist, so I wasn't convinced of his knowledge of mushrooms. Also, I'd hate to be the one who killed a friend with bad drugs.

Even Estonians can sometimes get it wrong. My wife Liina's friend Tiina called several weeks ago, asking us if we wanted to go mushrooming. We were busy painting the house that day and had to say no.

The next day Tiina called from the hospital. She's made a fresh mushroom sauce to go on her pasta, and it turned out she'd picked the wrong sort. "The doctor says I'm lucky my three-year-old son didn't eat them," she reported to Liina. I continued painting the house, this time with new vigor, grateful to the sticky white paint which had spared me a miserable fate.

Liina disappeared into the house with the phone, consoling her friend, but surely quite happy that she hadn't gone mushrooming. Later, I saw Liina walking to the car dressed entirely in white. On her head she wore a giant red beret which she'd covered with small white spots of paper. "Wanna come?" she asked.

"Where?"

"To visit Tiina in the hospital." Liina roamed around our garden, gathering any kind of mushroom she saw, even plucking them off trees until she had filled a small sandwich bag.

I tried to imagine myself in Tiina's place in the hospital. I wondered if I'd find it funny if a friend showed up dressed as a giant fly agaric with a sack full of fungus as a gift. I thought I probably wouldn't.

I told Liina I'd continue painting the house. And then I thought of Poolseitse. Poolseitse would find it funny. She would have howled at the sight of an arrogant and ignorant city girl filling her sack with suspect mushrooms and preparing a gourmet poison pasta sauce in a two-hundred-dollar pan.

"Hey," I said to Liina, as she was about to get in the car. "I *will* come with you. But only if you've got another one of those berets." Liina smiled. She said she could come up with something.

❸❻ What Crisis?

Every day I read about Estonia's economic crisis. The newspaper says loans are hard to get and thirty percent of restaurants may close by spring. And there's a story circulating about Estonians smashing their luxury cars into trees, collecting the insurance, and buying more modest vehicles. I've read about falling apartment prices and the greater need for owners to get rental income from empty flats. But I've only read about the crisis. I'm still waiting for personal anecdotal evidence to catch up with the papers.

A friend of mine, a well-known French writer named Guillaume, recently moved to Tallinn. He wanted a quiet place to spend a year finishing his next book, and Tallinn fit the bill: a fairytale city mostly undiscovered by the rest of the world. He searched the web, found a beautiful place in the Old Town, and called up the listed agent.

"You want to see it *today*?" the agent asked.

"Yes," he said. "I'm ready to rent."

"What about next week?" the agent offered. "Why don't you call me back then."

A bit puzzled, Guillaume conveyed the information to my wife. Liina took the phone from him. "I don't understand," she said in Estonian. "This guy's ready to rent today. The apartment is available. You're even advertising it. This is the easiest money you'll make this year, and you want to wait until next week?

There was a pause on the agent's end of the line. Then: "Are you making fun of me?"

Liina turned to us. "He wants to know if we're making fun of him." We burst into laughter so loud the agent couldn't have helped but hear. We honestly weren't making fun of him. At least not before he made The Most Asinine Remark of This Century.

"We're not making fun of you," Liina told him, trying to choke back laughter. "But this guy is ready to move in immediately. He's motivated." Actually, it was Liina who was motivated. Guillaume had been sleeping on our couch for several days. He's a good friend, but even friends wear out their welcome when they're making camp in the middle of your living room. The agent's end of the line remained silent. Perhaps he was thinking about how he might kill us and stash the bodies under the apartment floorboards. Or maybe, we hoped, he was entertaining rational thoughts and might deign to do his job and show an apartment. Liina pushed him a little more. "How many people do you have ready to pay the prices you're asking for Old Town flats?"

"Let me think about it," came the reply.

Liina hung up the phone. The agent could think as much as he wanted. Liina had already thought about it. "You're not going to get that apartment, Guillaume. Go back to the computer and find another."

Guillaume didn't understand. "It's an Estonian thing," she finally told him. "One of our strange customs of commerce."

The next agent we reached was taking a week's holiday and wasn't willing to show apartments until she returned. Liina asked if someone else from her firm might show the apartment. The agent said she didn't know.

"Look," Liina said. "Isn't better to get part of a commission than no commission at all?" The agent said she'd have to call us back. Of course, she never did.

Guillaume began to worry. He talked about moving to Riga. Or Minsk if he had to. Liina calmed him down. She explained that plenty of foreigners had found places to live in Tallinn. "Maybe Estonians hate me because I'm French?" Guillaume said.

"No, no," she corrected. "Estonians hate you because you're the customer."

Luckily, our third call turned up a broker who was willing to show apartments that very next day. Guillaume took the second place he saw and moved in the same afternoon.

Guillaume is quite happy in the new place, one hundred square meters on a medieval street. But he's still shaking his head over the quality of service he's found in Estonia. When he offered to pay to have a Xerox copy made in a hotel they chased him away because he wasn't a guest. "It's easier to get things done in Vietnam," he's said several times. He is very suspect of material he sees describing E-stonia and its forward-thinking people.

"You're a writer," Liina told him. "Don't you ever make things up?"

Guillaume is starting to get the picture. He now says that Estonia's real estate ads are better fiction than anything produced in 19th-century Russia. And he's looking skeptically at much of the other glowing things written about Estonia. "Summer," he recently exclaimed, "is another great lie of Estonia. They should be forced to call it something else."

Guillaume has been feeling down lately, and Liina and I are hoping things will get better for him. But if not, he can always spend time with us. And if all else fails, there will always be Minsk.

❸❼ Code Breakers

'**S**ometimes I feel like I'm writing the same column over and over again," I said to Liina. "Like I made the movie *101 Dalmatians*, got good reviews, and so decided to remake the film using Labrador Retrievers."

Liina just stared at me.

"You know, when I write about Estonian consumers allowing themselves to be screwed. Do you think that people notice the similarities or get tired of reading my pieces?"

"Well," she said. "For one thing, you don't have many competitors for your column. And secondly, the columns come out two weeks apart."

That was not the answer I was after.

Estonians often brag about how straightforward and honest they are, how they'll speak the truth even if it hurts. And how this is somehow a positive attribute.

When I was a kid, my mother had a cardinal rule for dealing with others: "If you don't have anything nice to say, then don't say anything at all." I still think that most of the time this isn't a bad rule. Ask yourself: In most instances, is there anything to be gained by saying exactly what you're thinking? Fools almost always know — or at least strongly suspect — they're fools. You telling them so isn't going to make them less foolish; it's only going to put you on their shitlist.

Liina believes that if you tell someone directly he's a shithead that he'll benefit and might even be grateful. "*Hey, yes, you're right. I am a shithead. Thanks for pointing that out. I wouldn't have known it had you not said it. And since you've brought it to my attention, I'll now rethink my shitheadedness and take constructive steps to be a better human being.*"

Would other cultures be better off if they adopted the Estonian model and spoke the raw truth? I'm not convinced.

If you happen to disagree with someone, it's more fruitful to get him talking, make him think you're listening, make him think you care. Then, after you've softened the beachheads with some nodding, a few "ah hahs", and a little pretend listening, you very gently suggest there might perhaps be another way of seeing the issue.

Liina claims it's a simply difference in languages. A direct answer to a direct question is not rude in Estonian, she says, but it can be in English. She calls English a coded language. For example, if an American is asked how he liked the food and he answers "It was interesting," this probably means he disliked it. (It at least suggests the host should not probe further.) If the same question is posed to an Estonian and he answers in his language that the food was interesting, then you know the food challenged his palate. Liina admits an Estonian wouldn't describe food with the word "interesting," but it's the best she could come up with on short notice.

"Raw honesty gives you a new point of view," she says. "How could you not be happy about it? Isn't that the whole point?" Well, Liina, thanks. That's very, uh, interesting.

But what's wrong with my coded language?

Estonians tend to attach gravity to the question, *"Kuidas läheb?"* ("How's it going?") I respect that, but I don't think it's necessarily a major achievement. For centuries, people in other cultures have asked "How's it going?" (*Comment ça va? Qué tal? Wie gehts? Kak dyela?*) as a form of "hello," and their civilizations haven't yet collapsed. When I answer "fine", I communicate that I'm grateful you asked but that I also understand you don't want to hear the answer. Because Estonians eschew that perfunctory exchange doesn't make them special. It makes them contrarian.

"Stop shitting on the Estonian soul," Liina shouted when I read her that last paragraph. (The reader may decide himself whether Liina benefitted from my directness.)

But if the "How's it going?" question is the mark of a coded language, then are not most languages coded? What then is Estonian's code? Is it really not coded? And if yes, is the fact it's not coded the very code itself? Maybe some sort of code might lend to more self-expression in Estonian society and therefore healthier living?

Liina argues that if I want honey from her lips that I shouldn't ask her opinion. In one respect she's right: I get good columns from arguing with her.

But maybe there's a happy medium between the two extremes, Estonian and western. Maybe Liina does happen to have a point about my coded language. When an American friend tells me something is "just terrific," I'm of course skeptical. Though when an Estonian friend tells me something is *"pask"* ("warm, runny shit"), I am also filled with doubt — it's surely not *that* bad.

An old friend of mine used to wear a t-shirt that read: *If you don't have something nice to say, then come over here and sit by me.* A wonderful sentiment, I think, beckoning those with nothing nice to say to vote with their feet, yet still protecting the optimists from a verbal haranguing. I ought to look into printing up several million of those for distribution in Estonia and the USA.

Liina can have the very first one.

❸❽ Life on the Small Screen

I n a routine dusting accident, Liina knocked our television off its stand and it hasn't worked since. Lacking the funds to buy the *de rigueur* flatscreen, we replaced our TV with a ten-year-old seventeen-inch model with rabbit-ears antennae.

After two weeks of the Estonian programs, *Reporter* and *Songs with Stars*, I've concluded that programs on channels 2 and 3 are not suitable for viewing on a small screen. Digital surround sound and a four-acre screen are in fact necessary: if the sound is loud enough and image big enough, it is possible to induce hypnosis and blind yourself to the programming. Our small screen just can't hack it: it somehow calls attention to the content.

Reporter is my favorite. It's a real art to produce a seven-minute segment on a broken sauna window. We learn that a jealous suitor shot it out (an otherwise nice guy, according to a neighbor), there was no one was inside (no kids or animals, thank God), and that the sauna owner was a woman (desired by the shooter of course). Or at least that's what I thought the story was about. My Estonian isn't perfect and sometimes I question whether *Reporter* is broadcasting the nonsense I think it's broadcasting.

Crime dramas are popular on both channels 2 and 3, and many of them star one of the lesser Baldwin brothers, which means the murderer can be identified by an attentive viewer within the program's first two minutes.

And then there are the movies. Channel 2 runs things like *Bad News Bears 5* and *Police Academy 17*. Most of these films are banned in Western countries by the Geneva Convention, and American investigators recently discovered that the CIA was using them to break prisoners at Guantanamo and Abu Ghraib.

Most of channel 2's other shows are of the quality of what Americans call "community access cable," which means that airtime is reserved for anybody with a pulse who wants twenty minutes to talk about the future of competitive knife throwing or do an abbreviated production of *King Lear* starring members of the local insane asylum. Channel 3 is slightly better, and shows like *Our Annie* (a cooking show) actually do help it halfway redeem itself. I say "halfway," because the host, Annie, will sometimes put a pork leg in the oven and then step out for a televised Thai massage. I'm not sure what massage has to do with cooking, so the fact that a spa gets airtime has always reeked to me of that particular Eastern European brand of journalistic sleaze — the "ordered" article or program.

Liina tells me the Estonian networks can't help it. She says they probably have limited budgets and are bad negotiators. I imagine the Hollywood rep to the Estonian buyer: "Sure, we've got that Anthony Hopkins picture you want, but you'll have to buy eleven Goldie Hawn films to get it."

Liina's other theory is that Estonian channels are secretly run by an old communist who can't understand English, and so he lets Janno Buschmann choose the films. Buschmann, in addition to being Estonia's most ubiquitous film translator, is also the man who gives us Stephen King in Estonian, and so I don't for one moment doubt the man's dark sense of humor.

Liina tells me that if I don't like the channels I don't have to watch them and says the reason I make fun of shows like *Dances with Stars* is because I'm jealous. "If they invited you on as a guest," she blew her top one day, "you'd think they were great shows!"

"Yeah, right," I replied. "My dream in life is to dance with Ester Tuiksoo and be known as Dancing Vello."

"You dumbass!" Liina retorted. "Ester sings! She doesn't dance."

"That's just this season," I fired back. "They all dance eventually."

But Liina might have a point. I honestly wouldn't mind being invited on *State Citizen* where I'd sit in an uncomfortable chair with my back straight and dispense brilliant advice on economic policy in my broken but charming Estonian. President Ilves might be watching, and he'd call up his friends in Brussels and get me a think tank job where I'd be paid 200,000 euros a year to drink Scotch and pontificate.

All my problems will soon be solved when the Estonian channels go digital: then I'll get none of them. And I'm waiting for that day. I'll miss the state-run ETV, of course, but Liina and I will both be better off without the rest. She won't have *The Bold and the Beautiful* and *Sturm der Liebe*. I'll miss *Lost* and *Gala Concert James Bond*. We'll be relegated to our books. And of course YouTube. Now *there's* a small screen we haven't begun to explore.

③❾ Taxi Trauma

When I first came to Estonia in 1991, I tried to be a chameleon. I practiced drinking vodka before noon, kept neatly torn strips of the daily paper *Postimees* in my bathroom, and forced myself to eat carp, even though it's a bottom-dweller that tastes like mud. As the nation developed, these habits quickly disappeared. Yet others remained. Estonians still remove their shoes before entering a home, song festivals still make me cry, and stopping for a red traffic light is still optional. With all the changes, I've tried to stay current and behave as a modern Estonian, with the exception of one item: I still don't like riding in the front seat of a taxi.

In New York, where I lived in the late eighties, nobody would think to sit in the front of a cab. The driver wouldn't unlock the front door unless you were a sultry *Vogue* model who looked particularly available. With few exceptions, passengers happily sat in the back behind bulletproof glass. Drivers were rarely models of good hygiene. If from the east, they often reeked of a spice bazaar. If they were white, they generally had the mien of a psycho killer and more body hair than a yeti. There were plenty of good reasons to ride in back.

But when I arrived in Estonia, I noticed passengers routinely leaping into the front seat of cabs without the slightest fear. In the early days, the cabs were mostly beige Ladas and the occasional black Volga. To enter the front seat of the cab was to enter the driver's private world. The factory stick-shift knob would be removed and replaced with something reflecting the driver's personality, like an animal skull or an enemy's finger set inside a glass globe. On the dashboard were stickers from foreign lands, or small banners with coats of arms from Estonian parishes. In rare cases, the driver had a bobble-headed toy dashboard dog from East Germany.

I tried to be Estonian and ride up front, but I couldn't help feeling I was violating the cabby's personal domain. It also seemed to compromise cabby-customer relations. When I rode in the back, I was being served. When I sat up front, I felt I might be asked to change a tire.

My place was in the back. Cabbies pushed the Lada's spare carburetor aside to make room for me. If they thought there was something wrong with me, they were polite enough not to show it. Their silence caused no end to my inner conflict. *If I sit in back,* I wondered, *will he think that I think I'm better than he is? If I sit in front, will he respect me more and cheat me less? If a Lada collides with a freight train, in which seat am I more likely to survive?*

I asked all my friends about this front-seat behavior. Was it a Soviet man-of-the-people thing that inspired Estonians to ride up front? Since we are both of equal value in a proper socialist society, would Marx want driver and passenger to sit side by side? This seemed plausible, since the Soviets took great pains to promote the common man. Kids wanted to grow up to be tractor drivers. Songs were written about tram drivers.

I spent years theorizing. Finally, my wife Liina got tired of it and explained that in a Soviet-made car, the front seat was the warmest place, so naturally the customer would sit there.

"Really?" I asked. I thought her reasoning sounded specious.

"Absolutely," she replied. "It's a well known fact."

"But Ladas are such tiny cars. The temperature can't differ that much from front to back."

"I have no idea," she confessed. "But you seem desperate for an explanation, so I gave you one."

I tried out my theory on her about it being something Soviet, about the passenger being the equal of the driver.

"What bullshit!" she choked. "I've never heard such nonsense." She said that Soviet equality propaganda might have been believable in Bear's Ass, Russia, but Estonians weren't having any of it.

For a while I put my theorizing to rest. I investigated other matters, like why Estonians wear their wedding rings on the right hand. Like why every Russian I ever passed on the street asked me for matches. You know, weighty matters.

But I've always returned to the cabbies. Just last week I stepped into a taxi in Helsinki. The back seat, of course. The driver was one of those avuncular Scandinavian types in a lint-free sweater.

"Hey, does anybody ever ride up front?" I asked.

He thought for a while, then: "My wife does."

"But what about passengers?"

"Oh, I get the occasional Estonian."

"Ah hah!" I had struck gold. "So why do you suppose that is?"

It was an eternity before he answered: "I've never really thought about that."

"Well, I have ..." and I launched into my Marxist theory.

He kept two hands on the wheel and looked straight ahead. But I could tell he was interested.

❹❶ Striptease

'I gnore the girl upstairs in the bed. There's a friend who's staying with me and she's his girlfriend." My French writer friend, Guillaume, was sitting in my car and talking on the phone to his Estonian landlord. He'd finally had enough of pitch-black days, and I was driving him and his boxes to the post office. His landlord was, at the same time, en route to show the soon-to-be-vacant apartment.

"You don't have a friend staying with you," I pointed out to him.

"Yeah, but I can't tell the landlord I've got a stripper in my bed."

"A stripper?"

"I met her at a club and we kind of hit it off."

"OK." I didn't ask which club. I mean, strippers have private lives, too. Maybe he'd met her sipping vintage Bordeaux in a local wine cellar.

As we pulled away from his apartment, Guillaume started having second thoughts. "Estonian strippers don't steal, do they? Maybe I should have taken my laptop with me?"

"Why don't you just kick her out?"

"Oh, I don't want to be rude. She's a really nice girl."

I told him I wasn't an expert, but from what I'd read in the papers, strippers frequently steal.

"Prostitutes steal. This girl is a stripper."

"She doesn't take money for sex?"

"God, no." He thought a bit and then added, "Well, not from me."

To make him feel better, I suggested that since she hadn't drugged him and left in the middle of the night, the odds were good she might not rob him. Guillaume decided we should drive back, and he ran in to get his computer.

"She's still asleep," he said, relieved.

"Did you take your cash, too?"

"I don't have any cash. She can only steal books, and she doesn't read French."

After we finished at the post office, I returned with Guillaume to his apartment. I wanted to get a look for myself. We passed the landlord on the staircase, and he mentioned nothing about a naked pole dancer asleep spread-eagle in the master bedroom.

She hadn't stolen anything from Guillaume. In fact, she was seated at his kitchen table, sipping coffee, typing away on her very own — and very expensive — laptop.

"This is my friend, Julia," Guillaume introduced her. She was tall and attractive. She was sluttier than a post office worker but less so than most of the high-booted girls you'll find prowling the streets of Tallinn.

I was pleasantly surprised. I've been to a few strip clubs in Tallinn and am always disappointed. The "dancing" is generally of a quality lower than a grade school ballet class, and often there's a shirtless male with a python who effectively douses any desire whipped up by the girls. And if the snake dance doesn't do it for you, the girls will often ruin the experience by rubbing their bodies against you and saying in a thick Russian accent, "You give me money now, da?"

I admit it's been several years since I've been to the clubs, and it's possible EU regulations have improved the dancing. But I doubt it. The strippers I've seen in Estonia were even lazier than construction workers. Since their clients were mostly catatonic Finns and undersexed Danes, they hardly had to do more than show up and get naked. The type of Finn we get in Tallinn doesn't expect much, doesn't speak much English, and so "give me money now" may really arouse him.

But Julia seemed different. She spoke British-accented English, was conservatively dressed, and had a contagious smile. We discussed politics and Europe, and she said she was getting ready to go to Barcelona "on business." She finished her coffee, closed her laptop, and kissed Guillaume on the cheek. She offered me her hand and wished me good day.

"See," Guillaume said when the door closed. "See what a judgmental ass you are?"

He was right, of course, but I wasn't going to admit it. "I'm not the one who ran back for his laptop," I said.

Guillaume and I drank coffee and talked about the sun-filled cafes of Paris. I told him I'd miss him and all his crazy adventures with people like Julia.

"But we can go see her dance before I leave," he said.

I told him I thought that was a fine idea.

④① Fair-weather Gentlemen

'W'hat invoice?" the real estate developer said. He didn't know it, but Liina had him on speakerphone. Phone conversations with him are cheap family entertainment.

"The one you didn't pay three months ago," she replied. This was one of her bigger clients for her interior design business. Around the house, I refer to this client as Snake.

"I didn't get the invoice," Snake said. "Can you send it again?"

That was three months ago. He still hasn't paid. I sometimes think that we should translate Snake's words to Latin and print them on currency: *Ego non adepto invoice. Vos transporto is iterum?*

The financial crisis has done a lot more than show who is, in the words of Warren Buffett, swimming without trunks. It's put a host of so-called businessmen under the loop and outed those who are in American parlance, "fair-weather" gentlemen: they behave as gentlemen only when business is going well.

Of course Snake got the invoice both times that Liina sent it: she has a collection of his "we'll get that paid right away" emails. So it's a rather odd dance that plays out on the phone, where both Liina and Snake know the invoice was sent and received, yet Snake claims he never got it and Liina, out of a combination of not wanting to call the guy a liar and the hope of getting her money, plays along with him. Wouldn't it just be easier on everyone if Snake would admit he doesn't have the money? That despite his Audi Q7 and Hugo Boss suits, it's really the bank who's running his company?

Instead, he's on the phone with my wife pretending he's a bigshot, talking about other gentlemen he's in business with, and trying to convince her to take on another project, even after he never paid her for the last one.

An even better question: Why is Liina still talking to him?

I've tried her to persuade her to walk away from the guy, to take their contract to a collections agency who will at least drag Snake's name through the mud. So that the next time he appears in the trashy tabloid, *Kroonika*, readers will look at his photo and say, "Ah, there's Snake again. Has no one killed that scumbag?" Getting the money out of Snake would be nice, but telling him to kiss her ass would be more satisfying. I can live without money. I can't live without my integrity.

Which is probably why I can't understand Snake. To me, there's no shame in bankruptcy itself. The shame is in pretending everything's going swimmingly.

But I doubt Snake's fooling anyone but himself. In Estonia's real estate heyday, my dog Mundo could have run Snake's real estate company. Some parts of the business excepted, it isn't rocket science to buy property, build ugly apartments on it, and then re-sell it. In fact, the greed and false confidence of gentleman geniuses like Snake is what got the world into the mess we're in. Why'd we ever let them run the place?

I think what we need in Estonia (not to mention the rest of the world) is a revolution of accountability. We start locally, because Estonia is so small no one can hide. Estonians seem to already know who the scumbags are in their country. But my question to you: Why haven't we run them out of town?

The first step in this revolution is the rule of No Second Chances. Let's say you're a university rector who spends the school's money on Church's English Shoes and a charter jet instead of on a student library. You should get the boot and never be allowed a second chance. That's right: Never. Not in a million years. Your ass should go to jail. And when you get out, the only job you should be able to get is shoveling coal into furnaces at the university you cheated. Well, okay, from time to time you should be released to do yard work, so that professors may point at you and say to students, "Look, there's the stupid son-of-a-bitch who abused the public trust."

The second rule of our revolution is Money is Not Your God. This could be taught by replacing obligatory Estonian military service with eight months of helping lepers in Orissa, India's poorest state. And this program isn't just for young men. Let's say you're a minor bureaucrat, convicted of siphoning off EU funds and awarding contracts to your own MTÜ. India will be happy to get the volunteers, and a little time away from fluorescent office lighting will do every public official some good.

Third is the rule of Public Humiliation. Let's say you're a minister of parliament who swapped land or sold your signature for cash. Public humiliation should be so steep that you'll flee to Argentina to live next door to Nazi war criminals (if you stashed a lot of dough) or in a tent on the beach (if you didn't).

Some Estonians argue that the reason these rules can't be applied is because so many who might apply them also have skeletons in their closets. This is entirely absurd. There are 1.3 million people in this country, some of them perfectly honest. Many have never cheated anyone, have paid all their bills, and will do most anything to honor their word when they shake your hand on any size deal. If you're an Estonian and haven't met any of them, then you need to crawl out of the cave you're living in and meet new people. There are some damned fine people in this country. (More good news: Some of these fine people are businessmen and some work in government.)

But what if the problem isn't Snake and his ilk? Might the bigger problem be the rest of us? Are we too forgiving? Are we too easily walked over? Maybe quoting Edmund Burke is overdoing it, but what the hell: "All that is necessary for the triumph of evil is that good men do nothing."

Some readers may wonder how I can judge. It's easy: I've never cheated a fellow citizen or stolen anything. And, for the rest of my life, I don't plan to. I also know plenty of rich people who got rich without stealing. So, in fact, it's damned easy to sit on my high horse and look down at people like Snake.

Yes, if Jesus were here he'd tell me not to be so judgmental. He'd tell me to turn the other cheek and give Snake love. But until Jesus arrives, I don't plan on forgiving Snake. And I think Estonia would be a hell of a lot better place if more of its good citizens weren't so forgiving, either.

❹❷ The Boring and the Beautiful

B rand Estonia strikes again. This time, the Republic of Estonia's marketing arm gives us: "Estonia. Positively Surprising." It's a slogan that's, well, surprisingly unsurprising.

I'm willing to forgive the bureaucrats for not knowing much about international marketing, but they could at least take a lesson from the movies. In *Crazy People*, Dudley Moore stars as an advertising executive who's reached his breaking point and, when committed to an insane asylum, starts to produce the best ads of his career by telling simple and compelling truths. Ads like these:

"Jaguar. For men who want hand-jobs from beautiful women they hardly know."

"Metamucil helps you go to the toilet. If you don't use it, you'll get cancer and die."

Moore also dabbles in tourism: "Forget France. The French can be annoying. Come to Greece. We're nicer."

But we can't blame Brand Estonia entirely. Give most of us tens of millions of dollars and the responsibility to promote Estonia, and we too might buckle under pressure and choose the most cautious route. Positively Surprising.

But there is still hope for Estonia. Brand Estonia may not get it, but others do.

Janek Mäggi recently wrote in the daily *Postimees* that Estonians want to be "the beautiful and the boring" and so offered some better slogans himself: "Europe's most beautiful women." For Finland he suggested "Northern Europe's Cheapest Beer."

Sadly, Mäggi doesn't happen to run Brand Estonia. Nor do I, unfortunately. But since my income is connected to the success of this small nation, I'm not above telling them how to do their job. So in the spirit of Dudley Moore and Janek Mäggi, I offer a handful of highly targeted slogans to carry Estonia abroad.

For Russia: "Estonia. The continent's closest flush toilet."

To the Italians: "Estonian women are too reserved to slap you."

For India: "Feel right at home — our taxi drivers will cheat you, too."

To the Swedes: "Europe's cheapest breast implants."

For Africa: "Come be stared at. But not necessarily in a bad way."

To Americans: "Estonia is Europe's low-calorie Russia: All the excitement with only half the danger."

To the Dutch: "Come touch a real live tree."

For Finland: "Vodka 9 euros per liter."

For men under 25: "A place where it's permitted to drive like in Hollywood action films."

For the French: "After you leave, you'll appreciate your own food more."

And to zee Germans: "Welcome home to the land you used to rule." Or for after the freedom monument is unveiled: "Europe's Biggest Balkenkreuz."

Of course you think I'm kidding. Actually, I'm exaggerating. But only slightly. My tasteless slogans may not be as suitable as Mäggi's, but there's a grain of truth in every one, a starting place from which a marketing message can be crafted.

In fairness to the marketing wizards at Brand Estonia, we shouldn't be so naïve to think one sentence is going to cause tourists and investors to come flocking over the border to see what Estonia is all about. Even one sentence plus a lot of money. Seventeen years is a very short time for a country to have formed any sort of identity, to know who it is and what it wants. When I was seventeen I was beset with conflicting goals: I wanted to drink beer and chase girls and show the world what an adult I was. As I later realized, I was bad at drinking beer, worse at chasing girls, and no clever slogan could ever have improved things. It wasn't that I was a bad guy. I just hadn't yet understood why I was a good guy. So perhaps we can forgive the shortcomings of a seventeen-year-old Estonia.

Still, though, if we're going to spend the money, why not get that one sentence right? There are plenty of good case studies. Recently, India greeted guests at the Davos World Economic Forum with a "Dream Team" (to quote *Newsweek*'s Fareed Zakaria) of India's most intelligent and articulate government officials. There were Hindi tunes, Indian dancers, and free iPod shuffles loaded with Bollywood music. Somehow they even talked the forum's chairman, Klaus Schwab, into wearing a turban and shawl. Their slogan? *India Everywhere.* "And it was," wrote Zakaria.

Good advertising presents a product much like a self-confident person presents himself: as he is, not as he wishes to be. Age seventeen is about the right time for

Estonia to look in the mirror and see who we are. To get comfortable in our skin and learn to be ourselves. And then advertise that. A big country with a big budget can get away with forgettable ads — put enough money behind even an inane slogan and it will eventually register. But Estonia doesn't have that luxury. When your budget is only a drop in the bucket of international media, you actually have to say something memorable.

Every time that Standard & Poor's or Moody's Investors Service drops its ratings on Estonia, some government official appears on camera to whine, "But they don't even know where Estonia is!" Of course they don't know where Estonia is. And at the rate we're going — "Welcome to Estonia" and "Positively Surprising" — they're not likely to know anytime soon. To them, Estonia is no different than Latvia. But hey, there's an idea in that: "Estonia. The Baltic State that Isn't Fucked Up." (Knock on wood, of course. Loudly.)

❹❸ Guilt Trip

Hard to believe, but in this economy a hamburger at the Radisson still costs fourteen dollars. That's far too much to pay, but it's the only decent burger in town. The price includes French fries and an extra large serving of guilt.

This recession has hit me hard — freelance writers are the only ones who go bankrupt faster than bad restaurants. Ordering the Radisson burger brought all kinds of guilt, financial and otherwise. Most of all, I felt guilty because I knew my wife Liina was home eating boiled potatoes. And there I was, sitting in the restaurant next to a street-level floor-to-ceiling window. I felt part of a billboard advertisement for some luxury good, the headline shouting: *I'm not sorry that I'm a rich asshole.*

Except for that I'm not rich. If the plague came to Tallinn, I'd die in the city with the masses, not having the means to afford a castle in the countryside.

I tried another mental tack to deal with my guilt. I thought of Liina at home and reasoned: *She's Estonian; she actually* likes *boiled potatoes.*

But that only partially worked. While I didn't feel like a rich asshole, I still felt like an asshole.

But, I thought, I'm not as bad as some.

A real estate developer I know forces his wife to borrow money from her girlfriends in order to pay the family's utility bills, while he himself somehow finds enough money for international travel. "Business trips," he tells her. Perhaps. But when he comes back he's always tanned.

My neighbor, a mid-level attorney at a large law firm, advertised his wife's fur coat on osta.ee, the local version of eBay. He snuck it out of the house and delivered it to the buyer, and his wife suspected nothing until she wanted to wear it to a dinner party. All evening long the wife talked about nothing but her "stolen" fur. The next day, the husband admitted he'd sold it but had said nothing because he didn't want it to spoil dinner.

And I'm feeling guilty over a burger? Strangely, I am.

Before my food even arrives I notice how filthy the table is. It's not sticky, but there are breadcrumbs all over it. For fourteen bucks... Yes, one would think.

Another lawyer I know, in order to cut down on family expenses, forced his wife to sell her car but then traded his own Toyota for a Mercedes Benz. When she questioned this logic he shouted at her, "Now's the time to get the best deals!" All I've done is buy a hamburger and I somehow feel like I'm in his league.

And then it arrives. It's a beautiful patty of beef complete with melted Roquefort cheese and four thick strips of bacon on top. The guilt momentarily subsides, but then I see the fries. Is that all? There are at least thirty percent fewer than in pre-crisis days. And they're not even fresh: they're clearly frozen, from a plastic bag. Fourteen dollars. And that doesn't include a beverage.

But the burger's so good. The beef is exquisite, and there's more bacon than I'd hoped for. It's cooked perfectly: pink in the center and hot off the grill.

I think about Liina at home. I've asked her to help share the burden. I still pay the mortgage, but she covers the utilities, the car insurance, and the groceries. I imagine her stabbing a potato with a fork and biting into it. I see her put it back on the plate and sprinkle it with salt.

I signal the waiter and ask for the check. The guy at the next table flags him down and barks "I'll have another." I want another, too. But I couldn't bear another. I'd deserve the heart attack I'd die of.

Liina, if you're reading this, forgive me. I've asked you to sacrifice and you have. Without a single complaint. I feel as if I've cheated on you. And worst of all, I can't promise it won't happen again.

④④ Veggie Quest

'**D**o you have anything for vegetarians?" We were in a café on Estonia's rural north coast and Liina was hungry.

"No!" shouted the woman behind the counter. *Shouted*, I kid you not.

But Liina could see carrots and beets under the sneeze-guard and just had to point it out. "Couldn't you just put those on a plate for me?"

"Those are for *komplektid*," she sneered, meaning in order to get a vegetable you had to order a full meal. She turned to the next person in the line, which just happened to be me.

"Don't you have anything for vegetarians?" I couldn't let her off without a fight.

By the look on her face you would have thought she'd been asked to gouge out the eyes of her favorite child. What had vegetables ever done to her? Had she been forced to eat beets as a child? Had her stepfather beat her with a sack of potatoes? I can't say she hated vegetables, but she clearly had something against people who ate them.

"Just replace the meat dish with another vegetable," Liina surrendered. "You can even charge me the same price."

I thought that was a pretty good deal for the cafe, but the worker obviously disagreed. She crossed her arms and turned her back. The international signal for *Get out of my restaurant*.

I should have flashed the toy plastic police badge I keep in my wallet and told her I was closing her restaurant for violation of EU vegetable discrimination laws. I should have reached across the counter, touched her softly on the back, and whispered, "Vegetarians forgive you." I should have done a lot of things. But those ideas, *l'esprit d'escalier*, as zee French call it, came later. At that moment I was nothing but stunned. What had Liina done but ask for some carrots?

It wasn't the first time she had been refused service for ordering only vegetables. Being an open vegetarian in the former Soviet Union is tantamount to being a convicted pedophile. At best, you'll be scorned but served. At worst, you're at risk for a beating. But usually, without too much of a fuss, you can strike some sort of deal with the restaurant.

The negotiation process can be intense. It often involves a long exchange with the waitress where Liina explains that being a vegetarian means eating vegetables. "Well, we've got chicken" inevitably follows, to which Liina replies that that's meat, too. "What about fish?" Liina then explains that some vegetarians eat fish, but she does not. She eats only vegetables. At this point, the waitress' memory will fail her and she'll offer chicken again. After a several minute process, the waitress finally exclaims: "You mean you only eat *vegetables*?"

Sometimes, the waitress will have read about this phenomenon in *Kroonika*. She may be aware that Alanis Morisette and Anne Hathaway are vegetarians. (Rarely will anyone know that Albert Einstein and Rainer Maria Rilke were vegetarians.) If you have a male server, there's a small chance he'll know Jenna Jameson, the porn star, is a vegetarian. But usually, even if the rural waiter has heard of vegetarians, he actually hasn't met one.

If the server happens to be open-minded, Liina often gets a chance to make her vegetarian case. She'll debunk the myth that you have to eat meat to get protein. She'll tell how she once got anemic and when doctors blamed her vegetarianism, she proved them wrong and got her iron through beans, lentils, grains, and dairy products. "But you wear leather shoes!" someone always points out. This invites Liina to talk about how we unavoidably kill lower organisms with every step we take, but that she only wants to minimize pain caused to animals. It's like listening to Gandhi (who, Liina will point out, was also a vegetarian).

It may be difficult to be a vegetarian, but what's more difficult is being a carnivore husband of a vegetarian. I actually like the cholesterol bombs served in rural Estonian cafes. Every once in a while, I love the classic country fare: a fat-laden pork steak, or *snitsel*. So every time we're turned away from some greasy country dump, sent packing toward a healthier restaurant (or worse, the local grocery store where we'll have to fix our own), I suffer a little bit, too. More and more, we end up taking our own food to the countryside, which means that, since I'm lazy, I eat whatever Liina prepares, making me a *de facto* vegetarian.

So as a vegetarian, I'd like to ask all rural café owners reading this to please allow your staff to replace the meat with a vegetable. Even if you don't give a damn about animals, your profit margins will be higher. And you'll sell one more *karbonaad* than you would have otherwise, since Liina's husband always follows when she gets thrown out on the street.

❹❺ Channeling Amy Vanderbilt

'I'm in meeting and I can't talk. Call me back in an hour." That's what I got when I called a woman who wanted me to edit her ten-thousand-word academic thesis for free. My response: "Up yours." Of course I didn't say it until after she'd hung up. And my answer had nothing to do with her wanting me to do it for free.

I've never thought of myself as a crusty old timer, but I am baffled by mobile phone etiquette. To my way of thinking, the woman answering the phone was doubly rude: first to those in her meeting, and secondly to me. If she didn't want to talk, why'd she bother to answer at all?

"But people expect you to answer," a friend explained after listening to my rant. "People know you've got the phone with you, so it's rude not to answer."

"What if I'm in the shower?" I countered. "What if I'm urinating? What if I'm on the table in the emergency room with a doctor carving out my appendix?"

"Well," he said sheepishly, "I've answered the phone in the shower."

And what's with this "Call me back..."? Wouldn't common courtesy dictate she call me back? After all, she was the one who wanted the favor. So now I was supposed to remember to call her back so I could be inconvenienced for her benefit? The whole situation smelled Soviet. Like in the Estonian government office I once worked where an unwanted phone call was silenced by raising the receiver a few centimeters from its cradle and letting it drop.

Up yours, indeed.

When I was a child — in the pre-mobile phone era — I was required to answer the telephone this way: *Vikerkaar residence, this is Vello speaking.* My brother and I hated it. As teenagers, it seemed completely over the top, like we were Canada farm kids pretending to be royalty. *Buckingham Palace, Queen Elizabeth speaking.* We had to take detailed messages, too, writing down the caller's name, number, and exact time of call. In the chaotic world we live in, it probably was reassuring when one of the Vikerkaar children answered the phone. But as with kids from any era, we were too focused on our own navels to care. But we did it anyway, because bad manners in our household just weren't tolerated. And dad wasn't afraid to enforce it with a belt.

In those days there were three doyens of manners. Emily Post, Miss Manners (Judith Martin's pseudonym), and Amy Vanderbilt. Our family's manners were guided by *Amy Vanderbilt's New Complete Book of Etiquette.* Published in 1952 — and seriously out of date in our household 25 years later — there were chapters titled "Employer-Servant Relations," "Ship Launchings and Visiting a Naval Vessel," and "An Audience with the Pope." But Mrs. Vanderbilt wasn't too out of touch. She knew that some people who bought books weren't rich enough to employ a butler and so included the chapter "Gracious Living without Servants."

Even though there weren't mobile phones for Mrs. Vanderbilt to write about, I think we'd concur on a few etiquette basics. I believe she'd agree that the man who answered his phone and carried on a five-minute conversation in the second row of the opera was not acting with consideration for others. She'd agree my neighbor who constantly talks on his phone while driving his Audi Q7 endangers fellow drivers. And she would note that if you indeed take calls while using the toilet, it is considerate to wait to flush.

With new technologies like the mobile phone where etiquette isn't yet formed, it is indeed our duty to challenge the devices, to consider what they contribute versus what they disrupt. *The New York Times* columnist Maureen Dowd recently posed two questions to the inventors of Twitter: *Did you know you were designing a toy for bored celebrities and high-school girls?* and *Was there anything in your childhood that led you to want to destroy civilization as we know it?*

Lucky for us all, Edward M. DelSole of Scranton, Pennsylvania, posted a solution in Dowd's comments section: "Don't 'Tweet' passively. Ensure what you're saying has purpose." I do believe he's channeling Amy Vanderbilt. I haven't been able to reach Mr. DelSole, but I think he'd say Mrs. Vanderbilt would have excoriated the woman who answered her mobile phone in the meeting. Mrs. Vanderbilt — an extremist to be sure — might have gone so far as to suggest the woman turn her phone *off.* Now there's a concept! Off!

Several years ago, I was laughing with my brother over the way our parents forced manners upon their children. When he raised the subject of our long telephone greeting, we broke out Amy Vanderbilt to review what she had to say. "A maid employed in the home ... answers the phone by saying 'Mr. Greer's residence' ... A member of the family merely answers 'Hello.'"

What fools we'd been! The long, excessive polite greeting was reserved for servants! Had we not been too lazy to read, we would have been well within our rights to answer the phone *Hello* like all of our friends. Of course, our jackbooted parents' logic was that answering hello led to soon answering *Yes?*, which led to swearing, which led to sex, which led to teen pregnancy, which led to your entire life being ruined forever. So I guess my parents had a point.

Maybe after reading this, the woman who answered her phone in the meeting will change her behavior. Probably not. Appeals for good manners rarely work without a belt. Which, come to think of it, I'll happen to have when I tell her I won't edit her thesis. But then comes the small matter of telling her why. There I'll just have to hope I can be as polite as Mrs. Vanderbilt.

❹❻ Spoiled Little Soviet Girl

Liina and I don't fight often, but when we do it sometimes ends with me calling her a spoiled little Soviet girl.

That's how it goes at the beginning of summer, when the weather warms enough that it's time for a new roof on the greenhouse, or the fence needs painting, firewood restacked, or a hundred other little jobs that the tough Estonian winter keeps us from doing earlier. "Why aren't there any kids around?" I lament, bent over a can of latex paint, trying to get more color on the house than I get on myself. "This is a perfect summer job for a high school kid." Then I'll start my tirade about how Tallinn kids don't seem to require summer jobs, how they spend their summers wind surfing or at grandma's summer cottage or just hanging out in a parking lot somewhere with an endless supply of cigarettes and beer.

Liina will reply that not every place in the world is like America, where all anybody does is work, and when people aren't working they're thinking about work. Liina knows that summers after my sixteenth birthday my mother shipped me to America, where my Uncle Feliks in Kansas found me work which, in my father's words, "built character." According to my family, Canadian kids were "soft," beneficiaries of a socialist system that encouraged reliance on the government cheese. If I went to America, the cruelest capitalist country of them all, then I'd be hardened and independent, never one to stand around and complain that the world is unfair. That was the logic, anyway.

My first American job was in the "building profession," as Uncle Feliks put it.

I imagined wearing a denim shirt and yellow hardhat, carrying around rolled-up architectural plans, and giving instructions to clean-cut men like those we see in deodorant commercials. Instead, I operated what is known to American builders as the Mexican backhoe: a shovel. And when I wasn't operating the Mexican backhoe, I ran a jackhammer. Once I spent an entire month removing a parking lot which a client argued didn't properly drain. Rather than sending out a machine that could destroy the parking lot in a single day, to punish the client the construction company sent me, a fifty-kilo kid with a twenty-five-kilo jackhammer. After thirty days of ceaseless noise and vibration I'd removed an entire parking lot in breadloaf-sized pieces. While I learned about character, the client learned what happens when you complain to a builder after you've already paid him.

The next summer Feliks got me a job as a plumber. Before I left Canada, my father explained what he called the cardinal rule of plumbing: Shit runs downhill. The job turned out to be more work with a Mexican backhoe, either digging holes or filling in those that others dug. As the smallest guy in the company, I was regularly called away from digging to descend into sewer lines with a plug to stop the flow of feces above a point where the real plumbers wanted to work.

Meanwhile, back in Estonia, what was Liina doing? She was windsurfing in the Bay of Tallinn and eating caviar from Viimsi's Kirovi Kaluri Kolkhoz (one bright exception to the rule of Soviet poverty) where she lived with her family. There are plenty of stories about how hard Soviet kids worked, how they toiled in the fields to bring in the harvest, because Soviet combines were of such quality they left forty percent of the harvest on the ground. Even smart kids sent to the malevs (a camp for elite kids, as I understand it) where I imagined them playing chess in the shade and talking about how they'd one day rule their country, had to do some symbolic work. A malev camper friend of mind once showed me a brick wall he built at a camp.

But Liina's summers were different.

When she wasn't "training," which many Estonian kids not destined for professional sports seem to do even today, she was aboard her family's Volga, traveling around the Soviet Union. She spent one summer on the White Sea, diving for starfish, which she and her family then killed, painted, and trucked south, where they were sold as souvenirs of the Black Sea. She argues that was a job, but I say diving for starfish hardly counts as work. Try diving for turds in a hundred-degree Kansas sewer.

Perhaps Liina is right about Tallinn kids not working. Maybe it isn't a tragedy. Maybe it is better for a kid to enjoy his youth before he becomes an adult and spends the rest of his life with a car payment, mortgage, and kids who need fed, watered, and educated. Maybe my father and Uncle Feliks were wrong in their belief that you can't understand the value of a dollar if you haven't earned it yourself. Perhaps they were wrong about character. Liina certainly lacks none.

But I was brought up the way I was brought up, and I don't think it will kill my kids to earn a little money to help pay for the surfing camps and general goofing around which I know their spoiled Soviet mother is going to encourage. Let my kids sell *Eesti Ekspress* on street corners or shovel snow off the neighbor's walk. Or better yet, let them go to America. Uncle Feliks has already offered to take them as soon as they're old enough to work. "America has Disneyland," I'll tell them. Little will they know it's two thousand kilometers from Kansas.

❹❼ Thumbing It

In North America, hitchhikers are one of three types: (1) Psycho-killers, (2) Soon-to-be victims of psycho-killers, or (3) Foreigners unaware of types one and two. But in Estonia, hitchhiking is not only safe, it's pleasurable, and it's one of the best ways for a foreigner to experience the countryside's natural beauty, as well as to meet colorful locals.

True, between the continents technique differs slightly. In America, the hitchhiker attempts to convey insouciance, even ennui. He stands one leg bent, gazing into the middle distance, thumb slightly off the hip, pointing in the vague proximity of the desired direction of travel. In Estonia, a more formal stance is customary: legs locked straight, eyes directed to oncoming traffic, arm extended in a gesture crossing a *Heil Hitler* salute with what is used to hail a taxi in New York.

In the early 1990s, I used the American style, until a friend explained that country folk might think I was sunning myself by the side of the road. Adopting the local technique helped somewhat, but so did waving a small Canadian flag, the international symbol of harmlessness. After that, I never stood long on the roadside.

Once I was picked up by a UAZ truck, its windshield shattered in a spider-web pattern. A couple of holes caused it to behave like a lung, expanding and contracting at regular intervals. "I can't go faster than forty," the driver explained. "Otherwise it'll cave in and cut your face." He had a beard like Rasputin, rotted teeth, and breath like a dragon. "Mind if I stop?" he asked. Who was I to mind? He pulled over at a kiosk and returned with three bottles of vodka that he rolled under the seat with a wink.

I never got picked up by hot, lonely women (as in the popular commercial for an allergy remedy). Most who offered a ride were truck drivers or pensioners. Both made for lively conversation and quick improvement in my language.

Several years later when I had a car, I tried to return the favor, and I picked up hitchhikers wherever they appeared. One cold winter's day, I picked up a young Russian woman near the Latvian border. She wore a light dress and no coat. "Don't you get cold?" I asked, eager to practice my poor Russian. "No," she said, "I'm fine." We drove a kilometer in silence until she finally spoke several long, complicated sentences.

"I have to say I didn't understand a single word you just said," I confessed.

She laughed, understanding that I was not Estonian. So she rephrased, making it simple: *"Seks, ne nado?"*

I felt immediately guilty that my minimal Russian skills had forced her into such coarse language. Surely, her original proposition had been as eloquent as a poem by Pushkin.

"Ne nado," I replied, but thanked her profusely for her kind offer. She indicated an area where I should pull off the road, and I watched in my rearview mirror as she stepped across the highway to work a line of parked lorries.

I imagined her knocking on a trucker's door and afterwards relating to him the anecdote about the foreigner who picked her up because he thought she was cold. Laughter would ring from the column of trucks into the still winter air. Undiscouraged, the foreigner drove on, eyes peeled for another hitchhiker.

❹❽ Economical Crisis

'**W**here else in the world," the young American asked me, "can you walk into a newspaper office and get a job on the very same day?" This was several years ago, and he'd just got a job at the *Baltic Times*, the region's only English-language newspaper. The young man had done some writing for his high school newspaper, but beyond that his chief qualification was English as his mother tongue. Before he arrived in Tallinn he'd worked a year pouring concrete for shopping mall foundations. His university diploma was in physical education.

"Does it worry you that you don't know anything about journalism or Estonia either one?" I asked. He had been candid with me. I wanted to return the favor.

"Just a bit," he replied. "But I figure they'll start me out with movie reviews."

The very next week I saw his byline under a story about Estonian politics.

The economic crisis has certainly bitten the Estonian-language press. Journalists are being let go or forced to take reductions in pay, magazines are merging, and publications are dying. But you never hear about the English-language press, which is completely under the radar. English-language journalists are being paid late or not at all, and the good old days when you could walk in with zero skills and get a job on the same day is, at least let's hope, gone forever. So when it concerns the local English-language press, a little bit of crisis isn't necessarily a bad thing.

Despite some bright points in Estonia's English-language journalism history (projects associated with Edward Lucas, Michael Tarm, or Steve Roman, for example), local English-language publications have mostly served as an embarrassment. Headlines like "People Having Less Estonian Babies," "Health Board Closed Recipe Factory in Tallinn Downtown," and this century's *pièce de résistance*, "Economical Crisis," make English-speaking Estonians wonder if the publications are not parodies or if all foreigners residing here are illiterate.

Part of the problem lies with the local owners of English-language publications. Some of them do not speak English at a level much above what's required to read a candy-bar wrapper, or if they do, they believe there is a direct path to ad revenue, ignoring the causal link between good content, readers, and the El Dorado of advertising gold.

One of my favorite English-language media moguls is from Vilnius. He has the habit of calling his employees peasants and kicking their chairs out from under them — a rather strange motivational strategy which, despite poor results, he continues to believe in. He is such a tyrant that no foreign editor has ever lasted more than six months working for him. I used to make a tidy sum sitting in his editor's chair for the two months it would take him to find a replacement. He wanted copy fast and I didn't mind producing it as long as he permitted me to write under pseudonyms, which I eagerly did, working my way through characters in the Snopes Trilogy. Few readers, I suspect, knew that Faulkner's lower-class rural laboring family could produce such readable copy.

Part of my job was to interview new editorial candidates. I would tell them directly that their life span on the job would be only slightly longer than a freshly-commissioned American First Lieutenant behind enemy lines in the Vietnam War. Most still couldn't wait to sign up.

What allowed me to keep the job? I think the combination of knowing I'd only be there as long as it took him to find his next whipping boy and the fact that we Canadians are tolerant and flexible enough we could probably work with Stalin, Hitler, Mao, Mussolini, and rest of the previous century's top baddies and still find something nice to say. Plus, I needed the money.

Oddly, this tyrant is also a very good businessman whose only indulgence seems to be a slick car, and his publications are indeed weathering the "economical crisis." Western news bureaus could learn a lot from him. He gets a phenomenal number of pages per employee, not that many of them are readable. It won't surprise me, though, if someday Arthur Sulzberger, Jr. hires him as a consultant. Western media appears almost that desperate.

What those of us who like to get the local news in English are left with is BBN, the English-language arm of the business daily, *Äripäev*. It's staffed — as far as I can determine — by one well-meaning woman who has the unenviable job of translating tiny bits of stories and then suffering the abuse foreign readers throw at her in the comments section. In addition to a glimpse of the news, BBN's website provides a source of therapy for foreigners as a place to vent, and often they rant tediously about how stupid Estonians are (and, by implication, how smart they are). One reader has gone so far to write all his comments in short non-rhyming stanzas resembling haikus, though their random structure would not suggest he does it consciously — I suspect his burning anger somehow causes his pinky to wander and repeatedly strike the return key.

The *Baltic Times* is still around, but since Steve Roman left the editor's chair I've assumed that in their zero-budget quest to make ice-cream from feces they'd replace him with retired, albeit highly-trained, circus dogs. But mostly I don't read it because I can get the news from Estonian papers, and because of my firm belief in the computer science axiom, GIGO (Garbage In, Garbage Out). If one aspires to write like Shakespeare, he won't get there by reading Danielle Steele.

I'm rooting for someone to succeed in English-language media, because I really would like to read intelligent commentary in English on the Baltic States. As it stands now, I'm left waiting for whatever occasional Edward Lucas piece touches our region. Although Edward occasionally fires an unqualified broadside (as he did recently in *Foreign Policy*: "It is a scandal, for example, that [Baltic] higher education…is so second-rate"), I have to forgive him, as he's the absolute best we've got.

Of course, towering high above all others is my English-language blog, but the silly names of our two-man news team (mine, plus photographer Imbi Imetore) don't lend a lot of credibility, plus we have a news budget entirely financed by Google Ads ($11.35 earned last year). Since Google doesn't cut the check until you reach a threshold of 25 dollars, both Imbi and I are still working on credit, which I suppose puts us neck in neck with every other publication in the world. So when you stop to think about it, we could come out of this crisis ahead.

But Imbi's let this crisis get her down. She hasn't made a photo in weeks. She could use a little motivation. Maybe it's about time I walk over to where she's sitting and kick her chair out from under her.

❹❾ Turn Your Head

Text printed on a tip jar aboard Tallink's M/S Star: *The more you tip, the nicer we are.*

Perhaps there wasn't enough space on the jar to fit what the bartender really wanted to write: *I've had a bad day. All my days are bad. The esprit de corps around here rivals that of the Gulag crews who dug the Belamor Canal by hand with shovels made entirely of wood. Won't you, please, thirsty consumer, go away and not trouble me with your business?*

I used to think it was worse in the USA, where the old rules of tipping have been thrown out the window, and even Starbucks employees (with health benefits!) expect tips after you've stood in line twenty minutes to wait on a long-haired philosophy major change his order three times and finally decide on a caffeine-free double grandé latté sprinkled with protein fiber powder. In America, there are tip jars in places like bookstores and movie theatres — as if twenty-five bucks for a hardback and twelve dollars for a movie isn't enough. Tipping is such a part of life that the Internal Revenue Service taxes waitresses on tips whether they actually receive them or not. After Broadway performances, where tickets can cost hundreds of dollars, actors appeal to the audience for additional contributions. Bloggers have "Feed Me" buttons with express connections to PayPal. Tipping in America long ago stopped meaning a little something added for good service. It's become an institution in itself.

Which is why I prefer Estonia. Like this country's tax code, the rules for tipping are more simple and straightforward. If you are pleased with the service, you tip a little bit, often just rounding up the bill or not waiting on your change. Servers don't yet feel entitled to tips, and I've even had instances where a waitress chased me out the door to return money I left on the table. "No, that's for you," I've had to explain, though this happens less frequently now that cruise boats full of Americans regularly dock in Tallinn. Damned Americans. They've gone and ruined this country, too.

But even in America I've never seen a tip jar as cheeky as Tallink's: *The more you tip, the nicer we are.* Just how nice could the bartender be? What is the upper limit of his niceness? Would "nicer" mean a smile? Eye contact? Would he give me free salted nuts with my beverage? Would he carry my bag to shore and pay for my taxi home? Somehow, I suspect "nice" for him means not sharing the negative aspects of his job with the passengers. "Nice" means he'll keep "nasty" in check.

I don't expect their workers to be nice to me; I just expect them to do their jobs. Which most of them do, in fact. But the tip jar goes too far. It reads like a Christmas-time message from UNICEF: *Just a few cents a day can change the life of this starving African child.*

I know the M/S in the vessel's name means Motor Ship, but the bartender's message makes me imagine shirtless, sweating Estonians shackled twelve to an oar beneath the auto deck, driven by a whip-wielding Soviet-era manager. He lashes at them to shut up about positive reinforcement in the workplace and row faster, those who slack off or die at the oars unceremoniously rolled overboard.

If I'm to believe what I read in the papers, then Tallink may not be the most employee-friendly place to work. The looks on their employees' faces would seem to confirm that. I understand they work long hours for little money, but so do school teachers and shopkeepers and nurses. And, even in America, when's the last time you saw a tip jar in a hospital?

But if a Tallink employee is dissatisfied, why can't he reserve expressing his displeasure for when owners Enn Pant or Ain Hanschmidt are on board? Why hold it against me? I'm only guilty of buying a ticket.

And isn't it, in principle, supposed to be the other way around? Isn't — especially in this economy — the *customer* king? It might be equally tasteless (and might earn you a gob of bartender spit in your beer), but it would seem more appropriate for the customer to hold a sign reading *The nicer you are, the more I tip.*

But I understand. I once was chained to the oars in the service sector. I was a stock boy at Kmart. My job was to clean up the aisle when a mother emptied the contents of her baby's diaper on to the floor (which, surprisingly, happened about as often as a Tallink passenger vomits in a deck passage). When I wasn't on diaper detail I had to clean the grease off the store's restaurant's hamburger grill, all the while dressed like a Mormon missionary in a white shirt and necktie. When I was lucky enough to be allowed to sack groceries, company policy required me to look every single customer in the eye and say, "Thank you for shopping at Kmart!" My boss, Mr. Siegel (whom I was not permitted to address by his first name) allowed no shorter version. A simple "thank you" did not suffice. I got out of there fast and went into the plumbing business. I still had to pick up turds, but I didn't have to wear a necktie while doing it.

My advice to the Tallink bartender: You've got to get out of there fast. Like Huck Finn, you got to light out for the territories ahead of the rest. Before Aunt Polly in her sailor outfit gets ahold of you. But in the meantime, while you're waiting to make your getaway, try to pretend you're not unhappy.

When I lived in New York I knew a 24-year-old girl who married a 70-year-old gazillionaire. He was a shriveled up, bitter old guy who was downright mean. "How can you stand the sex?" she was once asked at a table with friends. She raised her left hand to show us the three-carat diamond on her finger. "When he climbs on top of me, I just turn my head and stare at this rock."

That's what you've got to do, Mr. Bartender. Turn your head. And if your rock isn't motivating, you might, perhaps, look at the door.

🅵🅾 The Estonian Rovaniemi

Forget the Estonian Nokia. What we ought to be searching for is the Estonian Rovaniemi. I bow deeply to any town in the world that can convince tourists to visit by advertising cold and darkness.

I first heard about Rovaniemi in 1992. A Canadian family living in Tartu decided to spend their Christmas there, and so they drove northward to show their eight-year-old child, Charlie, the home of Santa Claus. Upon their return, they invited me over for dinner and for what has long been prohibited by the United Nations Convention Against Torture: the amateur vacation video.

For the two-hour duration of the footage, the screen remained pitch black except for the occasional trace of a street lamp or car lights. Sledding on Santa's mountain? Pitch black. Walking through downtown Rovaniemi? Pitch black. Visiting Santa's village and little Charlie taking a seat on the Big Man's lap? Pitch black.

While I went for frequent refills from the wine bottle in the kitchen, they remained glued to the screen. "Remember that, honey?" the wife shrieked. "Oh, yes, dear," the husband echoed. "That's Charlie coming down the mountain now!"

I was baffled. Had this family been drugged by the Finns? There was nothing interesting at all about Rovaniemi — or their video — but they were as hooked as heroin addicts.

Even now, having finally visited Rovaniemi myself, I don't understand the phenomenon. But I do understand that, if only for the sake of our economy, Estonia should have one, too. We've got dark. We've got cold and wet. What's stopping us from having our very own Rovaniemi?

My first thought was that we should simply steal the town. The government could hire a public relations firm to circulate the rumor that Santa has decided to relocate to Valga or Otepää. After some thought I realized this would be too easily exposed as Eastern European treachery. Better to kidnap the man, blame it on the Latvians, and arrange it so Santa is liberated by Estonians somewhere near Otepää. Having seen both towns, I'm willing to bet that, all other things equal, Santa will by far prefer Otepää over Rovaniemi. If not, we could line Santa's pockets with unspent EU developmental funds to ensure he sticks around. Then it's only a matter of buying some reindeer and letting them roam the streets as thick as rats in an Old Town sewer. Our own little Santa Claus village would be complete.

But my conscience got to bothering me. What I like to think separates Estonia from Eastern Europe is its dignity. Estonians walk taller, talk straighter, and, in my estimation, live in a higher orbit than the rest of the region. Estonia doesn't need a dirty trick. We don't need to scare the crap out of the world's children by kidnapping Santa. Forget the kids: let's scare the crap out of the adults.

He may not recall it, but some years ago Mart Laar, while taking part in a panel discussion hosted by a now-defunct English-language magazine, came up with the idea that Estonia should have its very own Soviet Horror Park. Laar has always been a man ahead of his time in his vision for Estonia.

Personally, I see twenty hectares of horror.

Once my prototypical Canadian family has bought their tickets from the gate attendant, they'll be stopped ten meters inside the park by an unshaven Russian *militsia* wearing an untucked shirt and a *forashka* on his head as big as a serving tray. "Sure you bought tickets," he'll tell the still-smiling Canadians, "but you didn't get them from me." So Karl Kanada will dig in his pocket for a few bills to ensure his family gets to see the attractions. In some cases, the family's car will be searched, the father's porn magazines and children's walkie-talkies confiscated. Alcohol will be removed (to be later resold in the gift shop or consumed by park employees) and a further fine levied on family members who neglected to purchase the park's special health insurance which was recommended to them at the gate, the policy which guarantees foreigners the "same fine quality of medical care available to citizens of the Soviet Union." (Incidentally, the park will house a small hospital where the only forms of accepted payment will be Levi's jeans and live chickens.)

By this time, Karl Kanada and his family will be extremely thirsty and will descend on the park's canteen, marked by a sign reading ресторан, at least half of the neon letters burned out. Karl will bribe the doorman, and once inside the family will spend hours deciphering the menu, finally realizing the restaurant has nothing on hand but pelmeni — and only *fried* pelmeni at that.

Exhausted, his hard currency nearly gone, Karl Kanada will take his family to the Intourist Hotel, where he'll be charged the foreigners' rate for a spartan room with no hot water and sheets a half meter too short for the bed. His key will be attached to a boat anchor and tended to by a *dezhurnaya*, who he will also need to bribe if he wants the family's sweaty clothes returned by the hotel's laundry service.

Sometime during the middle of the night, a knock will come at the door, and the family will be given ten minutes to pack and whisked down a back staircase into a waiting UAZ truck, then off to the park's train station where a Stolypin car awaits. "Wait, there must be some mistake!" Karl will wail. But the guard will turn a deaf ear until Karl removes his Rolex, his leather shoes, his wife's western brassiere, and anything else of value the family is carrying. Early in the morning, the family will return to their hotel on foot, to find their car stolen. "You only bought health insurance," the desk clerk will inform them. "You should have bought the auto insurance."

The deportation, being in such obvious bad taste, might be replaced by guests being rousted from their beds to be lightly beaten, then forced to sign a confession and inform on a neighbor — or, in cases of leniency, simply forced to write a postcard to their neighbors about the wonderful time they're having.

To me, it's a natural idea. It may not be exactly what Mr. Laar had in mind (I never had a chance to ask him), but it would certainly be one hell of a park. Educational for sure. Real family entertainment. The natural successor to reality television.

Vello, some will cry, you've stooped to a new low! How dare you make light of such a serious subject? I answer this way: Estonia can continue the frustrating search for its Nokia — or *seksikat produkti* (sexy products), as Prime Minister Ansip was quoted calling them in *Äripäev* — which it possibly won't find while anybody reading this is still alive. Or, it can take advantage of that which is right under its very nose. It isn't pretty, but it would be authentic. And thanks to Hollywood, with the West thinking that the Soviet Union was all about Bond and "Goldeneye grotesque," Estonia might be doing the world a service by setting things straight.

But there's Solzhenitsyn, Edward Lucas, and Anne Applebaum! a reader will protest. People know the crimes of the Soviet Union! No, dear reader, they don't. The masses don't read books and never have. Bad television and theme parks are the communication tools of our time. If we want to change the popular conception of history, then we've got to do it with Disney. Or rather our own sick interpretation thereof.

❺❶ Me and My "M"

Back in the 1990s, I did a favor that enabled an Estonian businessman to earn some money. The man had heard me muse about crossing America by motorcycle, and as a gesture of thanks, he offered to ship my bike — a Russian M — to any place I named. I chose Kansas, because that's where my Uncle Feliks lived, and because I knew how big America was: half of it was plenty for me. I would ride West to California and, as Hunter S. Thompson had done, "smoke weed in biker bars," "feel burning oil on my legs" and ride with the "rain in my eyes and my jaw clamped together in fear."

But anyone who has ridden an M knows that you don't ride it: you wrestle it. And so I spent much of the time behind the handlebars speculating about what the "M" in the bike's name might stand for. It certainly didn't mean *Mõnus*, though there was a decent chance it was *Mure*. If the "M" had been English, it would have stood for *Mess* or *Mistake*. But since it was a Russian bike, in all its foul-smelling, cloud-farting splendor, I searched my primitive Russian vocabulary. I assigned the "M" to Мучитель, or, since it was almost always broken, Мертвый.

What I had imagined as a romantic ride, cresting flowered hilltops, breathing pure oxygen, a busty blonde hitchhiker next to me in the mother-in-law killer, bore no relation to reality. Most days, I stood around in service stations in one-horse towns while American mechanics and their greasemonkey friends circled the M and peered into its workings. "How could we have been afraid of a nation that built this motorcycle?" scoffed a twenty-something mechanic near Russell, Kansas. "You ought to junk this thing and get a Jap bike."

"Actually," said a know-it-all sitting on a stack of old tires tipping back a frosty Coca-Cola, "that's a German bike. The russkies got 'em from the krauts as war reparations. Disassembled the factories, put 'em on railcars, and took 'em to Russia."

"Maybe so," replied the mechanic, "but it's still a piece of shit."

But it was *my* piece of shit, and I liked it. And the advantage of it was that it was primitively simple. Even though I couldn't fix it, most any farm boy could, and when a part fell off you could always find some local MacGyver who could fashion a new one out of something he found in the yard with grass growing up around it. I replaced so much of it that by two weeks into my journey, you could have said the bike wasn't Russian anymore. Sure, I still had to wrestle it, but it ran.

I crossed the plains of Kansas, stopping to visit all the state's superlatives: the world's tallest prairie dog, the world's largest hand-dug well, the world's biggest ball of twine, the world's biggest easel, and the world's biggest pallasite meteorite. All these places hoped to snare a passing motorist with a car full of bored kids. But my M trumped them all. I was a superstar. "Look, it's the Red Baron!" little kids would cry, even though the bike was black and didn't fly. Since I wasn't hairy, had no beard or visible prison tattoos, tourists did not fear me. They offered me cold beers to allow them to sit in the sidecar and have their pictures made.

More than two-thousand miles later, when I finally gazed at the ocean, I didn't feel the elation Thompson had described. I was dog tired. My body was caked with dirt. The ocean of northern California was far too cold to swim in. I forgot Thompson and thought of Kerouac whose goal was to piss into the Seine at dawn. The Pacific wasn't the Seine but the sentiment felt right. After zipping up my trousers I turned and walked away, leaving my M on the side of the road. Thieves and buzzards would be too smart to touch it, but a rider with a soul like mine might happen by. And it would surely call his name.

5 2 The Men I've Killed

'D o you know how many men I've killed?" It was our electrician. He often called around midnight and posed his standard question.

"No. How many?" It was my standard answer.

"You're not man enough to know."

"Okay. Don't tell me then." And then I hung up.

Most of the builders who've worked remodeling our house aren't as strange as the electrician, though they all have their quirks. I called up the door manufacturer to ask why he was late delivering and he responded, "We're building the locks right now."

Locks? Estonians didn't build the locks for those doors. I'd been to his showroom and seen the doors we ordered and knew the locks were made outside Estonia. And it wasn't like a special lock was built for each door. But I was stunned into silence by his answer. Had he been drinking? Did he really expect me to believe that story? Did he think I was some sort of idiot housewife?

Please, don't answer that.

All of the builders we've employed have been at least moderate drinkers. Depending on the season, I either find their empty bottles under a tree or in the corner of their tool shed where they sometimes go to eat lunch — "the booth" they call it. Usually they're not too drunk to do their jobs, but on occasion they'll get blitzed and install a window with the lock facing the garden or drop a sledge hammer on a freshly tiled floor. Then I have to call their boss. Usually, he just quietly sees to it that things are fixed, but once in a while he has to resort to fisticuffs. I've watched through the window as he invites the drunken worker into the booth. First, there are muffled shouts, and then the booth starts to rock like a ride at a cheap amusement park. After ten minutes, the boss comes out, dusts off his pants, gets into his truck and drives away. Later, the worker stumbles out with a towel pressed to his bloody face, and then we have no problems for quite some time. It's a special kind of system they've got. But it seems to work.

I've also noticed a tendency among builders to scoff at any work another builder has done. One builder describes everything as "porno." Porno means poorly built, and, as I've come to understand, is a gentler way of saying that something is FUBAR. If I ask about the foundation poured by a previous contractor, the builder will tell me it's "porno." The boiler the plumber installed? Porno. The weather? It's porno, too. Complete porno.

The English author Peter Mayle wrote a bestseller about the nutty French builders who remodeled his home. *A Year in Provence* made him millions by describing the foibles and follies of French peasant craftsmen. I've thought about writing about our experience, too, but when I try write something longer than a column on the subject, I become terribly depressed. I end up obsessing about all the money I'm spending to do jobs twice. I start to see conspiracy theories, imagining builders calling each other up in the middle of the night taking bets about who can get me to believe the most ridiculous lie: "Your doors are late because a UFO abducted the factory assembly line workers and they're recovering from anal penetration wounds."

Estonian builders employ the same tactics that Kremlin propaganda warriors use. They repeat and repeat the most far-fetched rhetoric until you eventually start to wonder whether it might be true. How many men, for instance, *had* my electrician killed?

The electrician calls about once a week, and every time I hang up on him he calls back in ten minutes. I try not to be mean, because there's the chance he really did see combat with the Soviet Army in Afghanistan. But I've still not figured out why he calls me.

"So ask me how many men I've killed!" he goads me.

"But I don't want to know."

"What do you mean you don't want to know?"

"Because I don't care. Why don't you ask me how many men I've killed?"

"You've never killed anybody. You weren't in the army."

"How would you know? Go on," I say, "ask me how many men I've killed."

"Okay," he finally gives in. "How many men have you killed?"

"You're not man enough to know."

And then I hang up. But give him ten minutes and he always calls back. And this time I just let it ring.

❺❸ Aunt Virve - in Memoriam

Iina's aunt Virve — immortalized in the pages of *Eesti Ekspress* for playing tug-of-war with a rabbit cage — died last week marking the end of an era. With Virve passed far more than a woman: to me she was symbolic of both a lifestyle and worldview.

I often recall her response when I engaged her in a discussion about politicians and bribes: "I wish somebody had offered me a bribe in my day." I found her response surprising. She was known as a maverick in the Estonian Soviet Ministry of Health, and her reform-minded bullheadedness won her а почетная грамота and почетный диплом, both presented in Commie-red leather folders with gold embossed print. Was it possible she had worked her entire career in the Soviet bureaucracy without being offered a single bribe? And would she really have gladly taken it?

In spite of her contradictions, or perhaps because of them, Aunt Virve was a living monument that all things in the Soviet Union weren't necessarily bad.

For Aunt Virve, time was a limitless commodity. She always had time for a discussion, even though you knew she was going to hold down both ends of it. I would sit and listen, and then, after a little while, I would sit and pretend to listen. While she held forth on the best type of pigtail and which open market to buy it, I would often study her old black and white photographs printed on the thin East German paper. She was young and vibrant with a smile like a flood, which, it seemed from holiday photographs, served to light the tables where she dined in Black Sea resorts.

She once talked about her suitor, Peep, who spent days lugging flat limestone rocks to build a sidewalk from the street to her house in the garden district. Poor Peep, I thought, slaving with fifty-kilo stones while she sat idly by with a glass of Kindzmarauli, telling him how to arrange them, or discoursing on the history of the glass in her hand — perhaps held by Czar Nicholas II moments before signing the treaty of Bjorko. She was an irrepressible storyteller. She was irrepressible.

Digging through her possessions after her death, I found her Soviet-era paper, *V.I. Lenin: the Dialectic, Cognitive Theory and the Logical Union.* I wished I might have discovered it sooner so that I could have asked about it. Was its public debut met with a rousing ovation? Or was it both written and received with a wink of the eye? And just how much time was left for treating patients after the obligatory rhetoric about Lenin's dialectic as it relates to medicine was finally out of the way?

Accurate or not, the West's idea of the Soviet Union was a place where millions spent their nights in cramped apartments teeming with friends, drinking vodka from dirty glasses and laughing quietly about the absurdity of their lives. In part, the West saw it as an era of silly slogans — *The Soviet Union is the Source of Peace; The Ideas of Lenin Live and Conquer* — and *Mir i druzhba*, grandiose toasts to world friendship. For those of my generation, the Soviet Union was a dysfunctional land run by overweight drunkards in fur hats, a place which would eventually collapse under the weight of its own silliness. But it was also a state with a hell of a lot of missiles, though there was no doubt Sting was right when he offended with his haughty verse, "I hope the Russians love their children, too."

Virve lived in a time and place characterized by some western writers as downright miserable. She had a Stalinist childhood with her sunset years spent in the abject poverty of a post-Soviet pension. A life lived in unconscious fear. Her lot to endure.

Though if her life was miserable, I never heard Virve complain. I never detected that she felt she suffered. She never sought pity or even understanding. She had nothing to prove or explain. In spite of her circumstances, she *lived*. And the evidence of this was her septuagenarian and nonagenarian friends — Urve, Evi-Mai, Nina — who rose at the wake and raised glass after glass in her memory. It served as a poignant reminder that regardless of what we do, where we work, what we accomplish, in the end we're left with nothing more than our family and friends. That modern Western cries for growth and progress matter no more in the end than they did coming from the mouths of Marx and Lenin.

Virve took life on her own terms and at her own pace. I only ever saw her rushed when she was on her way to Selver to buy cabbage or when a new issue of the free weekly, *Linnaleht,* was published, she on a mission to obtain multiple copies to light her stove. On the street, Virve put her head down and plowed forward like Stalin advancing on Berlin, her umbrella in hand, stabbing the ground before her and oblivious to the world around her.

Six months ago, Liina asked me to go downstairs to Aunt Virve's apartment and retrieve a pan she'd borrowed. Liina and I tried to time our meetings with her around the "History Hour" radio broadcasts or game shows starring Hannes Võrno — the only two things Estonia could offer which could keep Virve quiet. Knowing that Virve's health was fading and that walking in her door for anything was a twenty-minute exercise, I took along a tape recorder. Now, whenever I need to be reminded about what is important, I listen to her discourse from that day. The batteries died before she finished, but it's a classic filibuster about a frying pan, furry objects, and a ceramic dog from the Kola Peninsula. It might have seemed nonsensical. But if you listened carefully and patiently, and if you made the time, then Aunt Virve always made sense in the end.

PART TWO: LONGER STUFF

❺❹ Meet Your Local Action Hero

He was waiting for us on the island when we got off the ferry at Muhu. He was trolling for tourists.

"Hey man, you need ride?" he asked in English. I am easily recognized as a foreigner.

I said maybe we did need a ride, if he had no objection to the dog. But we had thought we'd take a bus. Island buses, if there's any free room, will stop and pick you up. They're relatively cheap, too.

"Well, dude," he said, "I am your lucky day." He asked our names and then stuck out his hand. "They call me the Tony." There are no articles in the Estonian language so those learning English often use the wrong one or forgo them altogether.

"Who calls you Tony?" my wife, Liina, asked him in Estonian, but he wasn't deterred.

"Everybody he call me the Tony," he replied in English. "My Estonian name is too hard."

"So it's short for Anthony?" Liina joined the game in English. "Maybe Antonio?"

"My Estonian name is too hard for Vello," Tony said. Despite my Estonian name, I was still a foreigner to Tony and therefore a linguistic idiot. I guessed his real name was probably Tõnu, and the only thing hard to pronounce about it is the "õ," a sound something like the "u" in "upper" but made closer to the front of the mouth.

"I have car, man. The kit car," he said. The driving age in Estonia is eighteen, and if Tony was old enough, it was only barely. He was about five-ten with a perfect complexion. He had hair the color of straw that he parted on the side and let sweep across his forehead in a curly wave. He still had his baby fat and his cheeks gave him a wholesome, harmless look. He looked like a kid who'd be used in a commercial to demonstrate the good effects of milk or to model Norwegian sweaters in an upscale American catalog.

"Will you take us to Kuuresaare?" I asked. "What will that cost?"

"Money, money, money," Tony sang, almost stripping my pack from my shoulders. "It's the rich man world."

"Okay," I said, "but we won't pay more than bus fare."

"You have the place to stay?" he asked, once he had us trapped in his car. It was a chocolate brown Ford Escort, the dashboard peppered with international stickers. Australia's flag was there. New Zealand. Great Britain. There was a tiny sticker, an image of a tree, that read *Vermont*. Dominating the dash was a large red, white, and blue bumper sticker which read, *Don't Mess with Texas*.

"We're camping," I said.

"Tenting?" he asked.

"Yes." Was that a word? Every time I doubt an Estonian's English, it turns up somewhere in literature. Like "more better." I corrected a friend once, noting that she should say better or best. "No," she said, "this is *more* better." Later I found it in Shakespeare.

Tony violently pumped the accelerator four or five times before turning the key. The engine ignored him. He did it again and the motor started. It sounded as if he had removed the muffler. Mundo howled. The inside of the car immediately smelled like oil.

"Windows open," Tony said, like he was a ship's captain delivering a command.

Tony pulled the Ford onto the road, jamming the accelerator to the floor, a dramatic gesture the car's power couldn't match. I looked for my seat belt on the passenger side, but the receptacle was missing on my left. "Note well," Tony said, and took his own seat belt and draped it across himself, giving the appearance to outsiders of two passengers following the law. "Pigs do not notice," he said, smiling.

"The pigs?"

"You got it," he said. "Pigs." He made the sound of siren and removed his wallet from his pocket. "Freeze," he said, repeatedly flipping his wallet open and closed. What kind of television had he been watching?

Tony reached below the dash and pushed a cassette tape into his deck. There was a lot of static on the tape, voices of people shouting to one another, and what sounded like hooves on cobblestone. Above the din was a female voice in what seemed to be German.

"What is this?" I asked.

"The information," Tony announced. "Tour." A harsh, guttural voice now worked to be heard above a car alarm. For all I knew, this could be a tour of Berlin.

"Is this German?"

"You have no German?" There was disappointment in his voice.

"No," I said. "No German."

"You also no German?" he asked Liina and Mundo in the backseat.

"Nein," said Liina. "Zee girl no German."

"Fuck," said Tony. He removed the tape and set it gently on the dash.

"Don't worry about it. It's not that bad," I said.

"Fuckin' A," he said.

I've never known what that means. In some contexts, I think it adds emphasis, as in "boy, you said it." Sometimes, I think it means simply "yes." I don't know. Because of this doubt, I don't think I've ever used it.

I looked over and Tony gave me a big smile and a thumbs-up sign.

"USA, right on," he said. He retracted his thumb and reached into his pocket and offered me a cigarette. "Camel?"

"No," I said. "Thanks."

"Mind if I smoke?" he asked. "Mind if I fart?" He laughed hard to himself and lit a cigarette. "Americans do not smoke?"

I shook my head. I couldn't help but laugh, too.

"Where is your home?"

"Canada," I replied.

"Not California, USA?" He seemed disappointed not to have picked up a Californian. "California is the big place."

"Yes," I said. "My home is smaller." When I lived in Estonia in the early 1990s, I used to tell people I was from New York. It's where I had lived before moving to Estonia. I'm sure I took a bit of pride in saying that, and I couldn't have said Scarborough (the Toronto neighborhood where I was born and raised) because everybody would have just said "What?" At least, that's what everybody in New York said. "Have you heard of Scarborough?" I asked.

"Fuck no," he said. I admired his honesty.

"You don't have to say fuck all the time," I said. "We don't really use it all that much in conversation." I liked Tony. It was hard not to want to do him a favor.

Tony yanked at the wheel and the car suddenly shot off the road into the parking lot of a gas station. Mundo fell against Liina in the back seat, she hugging him to keep him upright. Tony stood on the brakes and the car skidded ten feet to a stop on the gravel parking lot.

"Fuck," Liina shouted. "That's fucking driving!"

"Moment!" Tony threw open his door and shot for the station door.

Liina and I had a few words about encouraging him. She told me to relax, that it was unlikely he'd ever be made Estonian Ambassador to the United States. I also expressed my suspicions that we were being shanghaied into some tourist situation. She again told me to shut up and relax.

A few minutes later, Tony bounded smiling out the station door, his golden hair bouncing like in a shampoo commercial. "There you are," he said, reaching through the window to hand me a bottle of beer, grabbing it back at the last moment to pop its cap with the business end of his cigarette lighter. "Sorry," he smiled. He reached down for the hood release, and skipped around to the front of his car where he added a quart of oil. "Kit loves an oil," he shouted.

"This is a kit car?" I asked Liina in English, having no idea the word for kit in Estonian. Who would make a kit car to look like an Escort? No way was this a kit car.

"What's a kit car?" she asked.

"Kit cars are cars you put together yourself," I explained. "Maybe Tony just pimped it up and thinks it's a kit car." But what had he done to pimp it up? He didn't even have an air freshener.

Tony closed the hood and threw away the oil can.

"Turkey sex," he said, climbing into the car and taking a beer out of his pocket. It's how they tell foreigners to remember *terviseks*. *Terviseks* is literally "to your health," but everyone makes special note of the ending.

"Fuckin' A," I said, getting into the spirit of things. It was good beer, too. Saaremaa beer. Made locally on the island. "What do I owe you?" I asked him. "For the beer."

Tony smiled hugely and waved me off, pumping the accelerator several times and starting the motor.

"So the pigs don't care if you drink and drive?" I asked him.

"You got it," he said, gave me a thumbs-up sign, and floored it again, grimacing as if waiting for the G-forces that never came.

Liina reached forward and borrowed my beer. She took a sip and poured a little in her palm for Mundo.

"Fucking Kuuresaare," Tony said. "You going to the Kuuresaare?"

"Right," I said. "We're catching the Ruhnu ferry tomorrow." We were going to visit Liina's father, Ruhnu Island's former military governor.

"Tenting tonight, yes?" he asked. I was pleased he hadn't forgotten that.

"I know the good tenting place," he said. "Fucking good place."

Thirty minutes later, we skidded to a stop in a quiet residential neighborhood in Kuuresaare. Outside the car were a series of black marks where Tony had probably burned rubber, practicing parking maneuvers he'd seen on *The Dukes of Hazzard*. We stood in front of a two-story, cream-colored house. "Most best tenting in Kuuresaare," he said. He showed us around back to the garden where there was soft green grass, two apple trees, several gooseberry bushes, and tomato plants in a small greenhouse. Mundo lay on his back and rolled in the grass.

"Put things here," said Tony. "We go inside."

A window opened on the second floor and an elderly woman stuck her head out. "What a beautiful dog," she said in Estonian. "Which breed is that?"

Liina struck up a conversation with her while Tony took me inside. We removed our shoes as is customary and Tony took me upstairs.

"My grandmother," he said, knocking on a door. The old woman beckoned and we entered. "This is Vello," Tony said in Estonian. He's from America.

"Actually, Canada," I said, shaking his grandmother's hand. Her name was Margarita, but she went by Margit.

"Your Estonian is very good," she said.

"Well, I've only said three words," I demurred.

"And now a few more," she smiled. She was clearly Tony's kin. She was not only charming but stunning. She looked trim and fit, although she moved with a cane in her left hand. Her hair was pure white which she wore in a bun. On her left index finger she wore a large sapphire ring. "And you are the dog's master," she said, looking behind me. Liina had left Mundo in the yard to join us.

"And the wife of this man," she said, taking the grandmother's hand.

"Then you've all done well," she said. She was treating us as if we were no imposition. Like we'd been expected.

"Come on," Tony said to me in English. "Follow me. We come back to here."

I excused myself and Margit and Liina fell into conversation like they'd known each other years.

"Your Estonian is good," Tony said in English. "But I need a practice."

"Just practice," I corrected.

"You got it," he said.

Tony led me down the stairs. "Grandmother lives in the upstairs. I live in the downstairs." We entered a room with a large television and speakers, a DVD player, and a vast library of movies. Tony owned just about every action movie ever made. "This way I learn English," Tony said.

"So I fucking understand," I said, hoping he'd get my joke.

Tony laughed.

"Where did you get all the tapes?" I asked.

"Black market," he said. "Cheap. You like the movies?"

"I listen more to music."

"Who you like?"

"Most anything. Some Clapton. Tom Waits."

"Ah, Clapton," he said, and walked to a wall full of CDs. He searched for a minute and then handed me one from the rack. *Eric Clapton Super Best*, the cover read.

"I don't think I've seen this one," I said.

"Yes," he laughed. "Very special."

"You sleep in here?"

"Sleep in here," he said, leading me into another room.

His bedroom walls were covered with posters. On one wall was a leather-jacketed David Hasselhoff giving a thumbs-up in front of a black Pontiac TransAm. The English copy read *You got it!* On another wall was a framed, plug-in poster of the TransAm, a red light continually cycled from left to right. The copy read, *KITT: Knight Industries Two Thousand*. A third one, a close-up of Hasselhoff, had text I couldn't understand.

"I can't read that one," I said.

"It's Finnish," he said. "Estonian is *Rüütel äss*."

"Knight Ace," I said. "But we called him Knight Rider. I've heard he has a singing career in Germany."

"He is a fucking bad singer," said Tony. "But he has the cool car."

Tony's grandmother shouted at us from upstairs.

"Grandmother takes tea," he said. "We go."

"Has Tony been practicing his English with you?" Grandmother asked me, pouring tea and offering me small open-faced sandwiches.

"His English is good," I said.

"Oh, don't flatter," Grandmother said in English. "It isn't at all good." It was flawless American English. Completely without accent.

"Well," I backpedaled, stunned by her English. "He does tend to use a lot of idioms."

"Ghetto idioms." She looked at Tony. "Do you even know what an idiom is?"

Tony gave her a sheepish look.

"You speak like a Negro in a street gang."

"Where did you learn your English?" I attempted to run cover for Tony.

"In Moscow," she said. "At the language institute."

I immediately thought KGB. I'd met several Russian army officers who had been trained there. They also spoke flawless English, though with British accents. I imagined Grandma Margit as a mole in our defense department, answering phones by day in her perfect American English and photographing her boss's files by night with a Minox camera. "How did you learn the American accent?"

"I had an American instructor." Of course she did. Some American Kim Philby. "We also had movies. *Roman Holiday* was my favorite."

I'd seen that one dubbed in Russian, and it had made an impression on me, too, although the film probably meant different things to the two of us. To Grandmother, it probably represented the lying, duplicitous nature of American journalists and European royalty. For me, it meant freedom from bad dubbing. In post-Soviet years, the Russians used one male voiceover who shouted all the parts — male and female — over the original dialogue, so it was a real treat to see an old film professionally dubbed. But there was a 90-minute rule, or so I was told. Films that ran over the time limit were simply cut short. That's how it was with *Roman Holiday.* They cut the dramatic ending where Cary Grant meets Audrey Hepburn and they come to terms with their real-life obligations. Maybe Grandmother had never seen it either: it was probably edited out at the institute so as not to complicate ideological lessons. It was a beautiful film, though, beautifully dubbed using separate voices for each character, and they'd hacked the end off of it. Someone later told me there was no such thing as a 90-minute rule, so maybe my film just broke.

"The Tony has movies, too," Grandmother added with a punishing glance his way.

"Well, maybe he could do with better quality movies," I suggested.

"An understatement, young man."

I wondered if we weren't pawns in some great conspiracy. Shanghaied by an elderly spy for the purposes of brain washing Tony.

"He calls himself The Tony," she said. "No respect for the article. And his name isn't even close to Tony."

"What is it?" I asked. I wanted to defend him, but I was also curious.

"Aare," she said.

We all burst into laughter. Tony included. Aare is a common Estonian male name. It translates as *Treasure.*

"I think Tony is a fine name," I said.

"For Italian thugs," Grandmother added.

"My father's name is Tony." I tried to keep a straight face.

Grandmother half-smiled at me. "For Americans," she said. "It's a fine name."

Liina had been sitting silently, reluctant to speak. She is shy about her English, although it was far better than Tony's. Grandmother was a gracious host and switched back to Estonian.

"And you?" she asked Liina. "Have you taken an American name?"

"They call me *Leee-na*," she said, making the first syllable about twice as long as it would be in Estonian. "When they see it on my CV they think I'm black."

"Well, Tony wants to be black." Grandmother was relentless.

"When we get home, I'm going to send Tony some better movies," I announced, hoping Grandmother might back off. "But right now, may I give a piece of ham to our dog?"

"Oh, my, of course." Grandmother scrambled like a host who'd forgotten a guest. She filled a plate with several slices. "I'll take it down to him at once."

"That isn't necessary," said Liina, rising, taking the plate from Grandmother. "We'll do it."

Tony led the way down the stairs. He paused on the stoop. "My English is not the same bad as she says." It was more of a question than a statement.

"No," I said. "She was a bit hard on you." I expected a *Fuckin' A* or *You got it!* or at least a thumbs up. But he had a serious mien. "Actually, Tony," I said. "Your English should be a lot better, considering your teacher." Estonians are suspicious of compliments, always looking for your real motive. So I figured I had to level with him.

He looked at his feet.

"Pay some attention to how people really talk," I said. "Read a book, maybe."

Yes, he nodded. Maybe he would read a book. "Thank you," he said, brightening a bit, as if maybe my idea wasn't so terrible. He offered me his hand and we shook goodnight.

Tony left and we pitched the tent under an apple tree. Grandmother called down from the window and offered for us to sleep inside, but we were comfortable and accustomed to the tent. As I thought about her she became even more mysterious. It was a rare Estonian who was sent to Moscow to study languages. After the Russians invaded the country, they reduced Estonia's population by one third through executions, one-way trips to Siberia, and emigration. Estonians weren't trusted to make good spies. Maybe she'd done what was necessary to stay alive. Maybe she'd believed in communism. Of course, maybe I was just inventing things. All she'd done was learn English in Moscow. That didn't make her a spy.

Later, Grandmother came down and said she wouldn't be home when we left in the morning and wanted to say goodbye now. I wanted to ask her questions, but she'd been such a good host, and I couldn't bring myself to pry. She gave each of us a hug and wished us good travels. She scratched Mundo's belly and brought him a plate of ham and a few slices of cheese. We slept well.

The next morning, Tony loaded our bags in KITT and drove us to the Ruhnu ferry.

"What do I owe you, Tony?" I asked as he shook our hands.

"Nothing," he said, raising his hands in a defensive gesture. "Please."

"Okay, but I'm going to send you some movies," I said.

"Yes, thank you," he said, shaking my hand again.

I meant it, too. As we waved to Tony and boarded the ferry, I compiled a mental list of the most violent films in which black men shoot guns, spin out in cars, and use fuck as every conceivable part of speech.

❺❺ A Quiet Man on Prangli Island

At night, from the rocky coast of Prangli Island, you can almost touch the Estonian mainland, the lights of Muuga Harbor gently illuminating warehouse rooftops along the shoreline. But of course it can't be touched, and for *pranglikad*, as Prangli residents are known, getting to the mainland isn't all that easy. For many, watching the Muuga Harbor lights is as close as they will ever get.

Prangli could have been created by a Hollywood set designer: Caribbean-blue water, alternating white-sand and rocky beaches, and fairy-tale forests. But despite its idyllic qualities, it isn't a place many choose to visit, and getting to Prangli seems as difficult as the *pranglikad*'s journey to the mainland.

Four times a week, there's a postal boat which makes a one-hour, return-trip journey from the mainland, but its motor has been broken for several weeks, and so it is moored at Leppneeme, the denizens of Prangli going without post, fresh bread, and visitors, which the boat sometimes also carries. Liina and I would be among the visitors, but since the postal boat is down, we hitch a ride on a fishing boat instead. It is a rusting, rotting 50-footer named *Püüton — the Python —* from the fleet of the former Kelnase Kolkhoz, built for harvesting *silt*, the sardine-like fish which is smoked, canned, and sold all over the Baltic and former Soviet Union. Instead of fish, the captain is hauling a load of elementary schoolchildren for a Prangli excursion, and for slightly under three US dollars each, Liina and I get a come-aboard nod.

Liina has lived much of her 32 years within twenty kilometers of the island but knows it only by reputation. Prangli children, once they reach high school age, are interned on the mainland, and the mention of Prangli to anyone on the Viimsi Peninsula activates the reflex gesture of the forefinger brought to the side of the head and turned like a ratchet. It is said *pranglikad* suffer from at least several hundred years of inbreeding.

Liina tells the story of the Prangli kid in her class whose Russian language dictation exercises were twice as long as anyone else's. His resembled a western union telegram: *BEGIN DICTATION MOTHER WANTS BREAD COMMA MILK COMMA AND BUTTER PERIOD OR SEMICOLON CAN YOU BRING PAPA SOME NEW SLIPPERS IF YOU FIND THEM TOO QUESTION MARK END DICTATION.*

When we arrive in Kelnase Harbor, youths on small-engine motorcycles and packs of mutt dogs surround the dock and inspect the passengers. There are only 120 *pranglikad*, and it seems many are present to welcome us, although this welcome consists of little more than a stare from a shirtless teenager on a dirt bike. Two drunks stand on the dock amidst the schoolchildren and watch as bags are tossed topside from the hold. Our Siberian husky, Mundo, hops ashore with the last of the kids, and we are told by one of the drunks to keep him on the leash.

"Set him loose," says the second drunk, staring down the first.

"He must be the mayor," Liina says in English, amused at their one-upmanship. "Is there a hotel or any place to stay on the island?" Liina asks him in Estonian.

"Could be," says the mayor, although it is clear he means no harm. His attention is simply focused elsewhere, waiting to see if anything interesting will be unloaded from the *Püüton.*

The schoolteacher is aware we have no place to stay and invites us to overnight in the *rahvamaja*, a large lodge, with the children. But we have no sleeping bags or mattresses, so this is out. We learned of the excursion and the possibility to hitch a ride at the last minute — and packed in ten minutes — so we lack quite a few items. The teacher suggests we follow the class into the village where we might meet someone sober. A young man along as a chaperone offers us smoked *silt* from a Styrofoam container which a parent presented the class. We had not had time to eat, either, and are famished. Liina breaks her vegetarian vow and eats the fish, feeding the heads and tails to Mundo.

There are twenty kids in the column ahead of us, none older than eleven or twelve, the youngest not too far out of kindergarten. There is an especially tiny one, dressed head to toe in camouflage, and he stays close by the teacher's side at the head of the column. Bringing up the rear is the man with the fish and his friend, an affable type in a red Benetton watchman's cap carrying a bedroll and a guitar.

The island is no more than five kilometers at its widest point, and so we don't have to walk far to find a sober villager. Liina sees him, too, and briefs me concerning strategy.

"You don't talk," she says, "until after the price has been agreed." My accent is thick and might drive the price up significantly. She is right for me to shut up: this particular villager may not be the man with the rooms to let, but he is likely related to him, and word travels fast about newcomers. We've seen no evidence of conventional telephone service on the island, but almost everyone carries mobile phones.

"The red house," the villager points. "Knock on the door."

Liina doesn't have to knock, because the man is working in his yard. The garden is freshly plowed, ready for seeding, the grass is cut, the hedges almost sculpted. Firewood is stacked neatly, right angles at every corner. Mundo jumps the stone wall surrounding the house and plays with the man's puppy.

"Sixty kroons," says the man. It's around five dollars for the night.

"Each?" asks Liina.

"Each."

"Sauna?" Liina asks.

"No," says the man.

"Breakfast?"

"No."

"Is it here?" Liina points to a small cottage separate from the main house.

"There," the man points back down the road. The beds are at the port, a kilometer back down the road we've already walked.

"Is there anything cheaper? Something not at the port?" Liina asks. She lived six months in India and acquired an insatiable need to haggle.

"No." The man holds his ground.

"Is there nothing else?" I suspect Liina wants the offer of hot water from the main house.

"No." The man repeats himself.

"Well, what should we do?" Liina seems to be addressing me, but quickly turns to the man. "There surely must be something else. Maybe a *turismi talu*?" She's talking about a tourist farm, a sort of minimalist dude ranch for Estonian city slickers who've never seen a goat.

"One-fifty," says the man, confirming its presence.

"Total?" This would be ten dollars.

"Each."

"Well what should we do … " Liina starts this again, and I'm unsure of my part. I was told to shut up, but now she seems to be talking to me. I'm confused about strategy, but I stick to the original plan. Liina tells the man we'll take the rooms at the port. He says he'll run get the keys. It's his longest sentence yet.

When the man goes inside, I tell Liina I'd rather stay at the dude ranch than the port with its oil stench and flea-bit dogs. She thought I would resist the ten dollars — I am, admittedly, sometimes cheap — and so took the port rooms. She happily chases after the man to tell him.

We get directions to the *talu* and find the owners also working in their garden. It, too, is as immaculate as a suburban Atlanta lawn, albeit more useful with its apple trees, gooseberry bushes, and large vegetable garden. My instructions again are to shut up, this time until money changes hands. We haven't heard the price from the horse's mouth yet, and although the man with the port rooms phoned ahead in our presence, it's possible he called them back later to alert them to a foreigner.

To make certain I don't ruin things, I stay outside the farmhouse while Liina goes inside to handle the business. I toss a stick for Mundo and turn around to find a woman staring me in the face. She's about my mother's age, but lacks my mom's friendly demeanor.

"Who are you?" she demands.

I'm doubly confused now. I have to say something. I'm not thinking fast enough.

"We heard this was a *turismitalu*," I say. "My wife is inside with the hostess."

There is silence. She looks me over, frowns at Mundo. She says nothing, turns and walks away.

Inside, Liina is explaining how 150 kroons each will cause great suffering. Before they went into the house, the hostess mentioned that a sauna would not be possible. In this country, on an island or not, ten dollars for a bed is outrageous without a sauna. Liina returns and reports she got her down to 270 kroons for the whole affair. "And I probably let her off easy," she adds. And she probably did, but I feel guilty about haggling over two dollars with a woman who probably needs the money.

The guesthouse is 400 meters from the main house and is separated by two fields, a hedgerow and a stone fence right out of Ireland. Given our reception here, I think of Frost's "Mending Wall," not the part taught in North American classrooms as a civilized aphorism, but the poem's general nastiness and possible allusions to neighbor killing.

The guesthouse is a simple wooden farmhouse with an asbestos roof — a fabricated shingle on which moss grows. It is probably close to a hundred years old, not at all considered old. The house's main door opens to a wood-floored sunroom with four chairs and a round table flanked by a particleboard china cabinet. A can of Cobra-brand insect killer and a Mennen Speedstick share a shelf with teacups and saucers.

I take a seat to contemplate its meaning and am startled by a man outside the door. "Electricity," he says loud enough to be heard through the windows, and he throws a switch on the outside of the house. I remark to Liina about the islanders' economy of words. "Yes," she says, and I don't know if this is a joke. I revert to my assignment, silence.

We make a meal of *võileib*, cold, open-faced sandwiches. We have butter, cheese, tomatoes, avocados, and for me, *pasteet*, an Eastern European sort of pâté, which to my palate is far better than its western counterpart. Mundo is treated to a jumbo can of Chappi, a Finnish dog food with an angry German Shepherd on the label.

It is almost June, and the Baltic sun will not set until after eleven, and so evening seems endless. After dinner, we decide to explore the island and look for a beach. Perhaps I will meet a few locals and talk to them, now that the room is paid for and I am free to talk.

We encounter three teenagers on the road through the village, and Liina tries out her island-speak on them.

"Where's the beach?"

The kids point in three different directions. We are on an island, after all.

"This way?" Liina points the direction the road goes. "What's there?"

"A church," the tallest one answers.

"And a beach?"

"Yes," he says.

"A sand beach?" Liina is careful to ask one question at a time.

"Yes."

"How far?"

This stumps them. They look at each other.

"In kilometers, for example," Liina offers.

They are somehow communicating between themselves without speaking, making a variety of faces indicating they have no idea how far a kilometer is.

"One? Two?" Liina gives them a choice.

"Yes," says the tall one.

We give up and walk on.

I've always found, without exception, that for every nasty, frozen Estonian I encounter, I soon meet another who shows great generosity and warmth. Once, traveling with my close friends Jerry and Christopher, we ran out of gas in unpopulated southern Estonia. We asked a farmer for some, but he coldly told us to push our car to the nearest filling station and wait. We did. Two hours later, when we were about to lose faith and open a bottle, the owners arrived. While Jerry filled up his car, I asked the owners about the river behind the station. Did it hold trout? It did, they said, and you're not from around here, are you? Jerry came over to pay them, and we must have charmed them with our heavy accents. We were invited into the station's back room, where they produced a bottle of vodka. Christopher, who lived in Latvia and spoke no Estonian save for *jäätis* (ice cream), made up names for each of the two owners — Father Nick and Horatio — and gave us running commentary in English while we drank. We finished their bottle, produced our own, and were invited to Father Nick's house for dinner. We followed him in his van. In the time it took for us to pry ourselves out of Jerry's tiny Russian car, Nick had lined up his family to greet us like heads of state. We shook everyone's hand and were ushered to an A-frame hunting lodge. Father Nick's wife served smoked moose and ham while Nick and Horatio told the story of shooting a boar between two of their gas pumps. Three bottles later, we left. Jerry was so drunk that he picked up a hitchhiker and made her convey us to our final destination. The hitchhiker was an attractive young woman who had had a fight with her husband and was going to town to spend the night with her sister. As if to put the cherry on the *jäätis* of friendliness, she invited Jerry to meet later for a drink.

But on Prangli, there is no such friendliness. When we walk toward the church on the far end of the island, people scowl from their windows and raise mobile telephones to their ears. Dogs scamper out from behind stone fences and growl at Mundo. It is as if the entire island has turned its back on us. I recall something I'd read, its source long forgotten, which would serve perfectly as the Prangli motto: *We do not know you. What is more, we do not wish to be known by you.*

The next morning, while Liina sleeps, I draw water from the deep garden well and make coffee in a pot that whistles like a winter storm. I drink coffee in the sunroom, warming my shoulders and the back of my neck. I read from *Across the River and into the Trees*, and the Colonel and Contessa sipping Valpolicella at the Gritti make my coffee taste even better. Mundo sleeps on his back, four paws in the air, in a patch of thick green grass. There are no sounds, save for the sea breeze in the treetops and the occasional hum of a motorcycle on the village road. It is a perfect morning for doing nothing but drinking coffee.

The village store opens at ten, and when we arrive for our provisioning, there is already a collection of locals waiting outside. They are three young men in their early twenties, one of them standing in filthy black jeans, a baby-blue windbreaker, and camouflage cap. The other two sit in fold-down cinema chairs, a row of which has been ripped from a theatre and deposited in front of the store. The three share two cigarettes.

"A line already?" Liina asks the one walking around. I have developed a habit of not talking.

"Heh!" he says. Not a word in any language I know.

"Are you from Prangli?" she asks.

"Heh!" he says again. We take this to be an answer in the affirmative.

"What do you do here?" Liina presses.

"We kill time with beer and vodka," he smiles, exhaling smoke and passing the cigarette back to his friend. "There aren't even any women on this island." Relatively speaking, we have met a gifted orator.

"Why don't you leave then?" Liina asks.

"Soon I'll have to," he says.

"Hah," shouts a passerby. "What idiot would let you out?"

"Where you going?" the orator asks. The passerby is walking with great purpose.

"The port."

"Why?"

"A meeting."

"What meeting?" It is good to see that the orator also has trouble extracting information.

"There's a ship offshore which wants to mine sand. I'm not sure if I'm going to permit it."

The passerby continues on his way and the orator explains that the ship needs the permission of the island's government to take sand.

"Is he on the council?" Liina asks.

"He's a drunk," answers the orator.

Inside, the store is slightly less Soviet than the outside due to its offering of western goods. There is a variety of canned goods, condiments, a large supply of plastic fly swatters, a selection of galoshes, one pair of men's shoes (blue running shoes, size 42), and two loaves of bread. Bread comes on the postal boat, and word is the boat will soon be fixed. And there is lots of alcohol. Behind the counter, to prevent theft, there are six shelves full of mostly vodka, flavored schnapps, and a few off-brand whiskies.

We are alone in the store, and through the window, covered with a typical faded green Soviet image of a milk pitcher, tea kettle, and drinking glasses, I can see the locals still sharing cigarettes and trading insults. Marching up the path, led by Mundo, is a parade of the twenty schoolchildren we'd sailed with aboard the *Püüton*. Right into the store they come, Mundo leading the way.

"No dogs in the store!" shouts the woman behind the counter. "They pee on everything."

"He's not a local," Liina says calmly. "He won't pee on anything."

The woman turns back to a customer, apparently satisfied. Mundo and the twenty children mill around examining chocolate and chewing gum.

After we stock up for lunch — they have enough goods to make potato salad — we walk back down the church road in search of a proper sand beach. We don't have to walk far to find a couple of boys on motorcycles. It seems motorcycles are the principal form of entertainment on the island. In the daytime, the island vaguely resembles New England's Block Island with its faint, ever-present hum of mopeds, replaced here by the more urgent whining of two-stroke dirt bikes. The bikers ride from the east end to the west end and back again. In case a Prangli denizen ever finds himself disoriented, the east and west ends of the island are conveniently labeled with expensive metal highway signs provided by the state. *Idaots* reads one. *Lääneots* reads the other. Eastern tip and western tip, respectively.

These boys are merely sitting on their motorcycles — perhaps to save gas — and it is easy to approach them.

"Is there a nice sand beach near here?" Liina asks. Again, I am quiet. I am invisible.

"No," answers one.

"Anywhere?" Liina simplifies her question.

There is a period of silence, perhaps thought. "Near the church," one concedes. We've been to the church and seen nothing but marsh and rock.

"Nothing closer?" Liina is more experienced now and isn't easily fooled.

"No."

"Nothing through those trees?"

"Well, yes."

"Can we get there through the forest?"

"No."

"What about a road? Does a road go there?"

"No."

"What about that road on the left. Does it curve around to the beach?"

"Yes," one says. "The road on the left."

The beach's beauty is staggering: water so clear you can see the bottom four meters down, cloud white sand with no seaweed, boulders the size of whales. We are in the island's lee, and there is no wind, just the sun's warmth. I try to swim, but the ice melted only a month ago. It's too cold to even wade, so I settle for washing my feet.

Liina makes potato salad, adding canned tuna to mine, and we snack on rabbit's cabbage we've picked along the narrow lanes outside the village. It has a sour taste, is often used for salad, and is found only in the spring. I prefer it raw, snapped fresh from the ground.

I remark to Liina that except for this beach, Prangli is not a place I would like to visit again. I tell her that I do not wish to make a premature judgment about the pranglikad, but that statistically, with a population of only 120, I suspect that our sample size is sufficient to reach a scientific conclusion.

"Did you come here to meet people?" she asks.

"No," I say. But on this island that could mean anything.

"No," she smiles. "I understand."

❺❻ Mundo the Adventure Dog

The sign on Mundo's crate read:

> *I am Mundo, Crown Prince of Estonia, Governor of Kõpu*
> *Peninsula, Rightful Heir to All Surveyed, and I am on*
> *a journey to reclaim my kingdom. I am 18-months old,*
> *friendly, but I do not like this cage. I hardly ever bark, but*
> *I like to talk.*
> *You may offer me food, but there's no guarantee I'll eat. I am fickle.*
> *Please give me water, although not too much, unless you want to get my*
> *master to let me out to pee. My master, Vello, who is also your passenger,*
> *is carrying all my medical documents, certificates, as well as some seda-*
> *tives, should I need them. My itinerary is attached.*

No adventure is complete without a dog, and mine's name is Mundo. He's a Siberian husky, black and white with a black mask. He has two white dots for eyebrows, which give the impression he's looking at you even when he's not. His eyes are a penetrating powder blue and when he does look at you, he seems to knowingly inflict guilt, reminding you of something left undone, like one of the rigorous walks he demands daily. When his ears point straight back and his tail wags violently, you know you've done something right. He also voices approval — or impatience — having mastered all the vowel sounds of both the English and Estonian languages. He doesn't talk much, but when he does, it's all diphthongs.

There are better travel dogs, certainly. Labs mind better, and the average traveler will not confuse them with wolves. Poodles, if you're not too proud to be seen with one, are cheaper to transport and require a smaller dosage of sedative. Border collies can learn more tricks and are conscientious about keeping your luggage together on the sidewalk. But huskies have a dignity the others lack, a regality that comes from their seeming indifference to all which passes before them. Save squirrels, that is. Mundo can't control himself with squirrels.

But in the absence of squirrels, which is much of the time while traveling, Mundo is able to affect Audrey Hepburn in *Roman Holiday* — "you may withdraw" — with remarkable accuracy. If Mundo pays attention to fellow travelers, he has deigned to do it. It is an act of charity, as unpredictable as it is charming.

Perhaps this is because dogs *know*. After hundreds of years of selective breeding, trying to remake them in our own image, more human, we have failed to remove instinct. Terriers no longer hunt rats, there are few bears left for the Akita, and the closest to a harness and sled Mundo gets is his leather leash and me behind it with a grocery bag. But still, Mundo knows. As a lead dog knows to ignore the musher's command because the ice is thin on the right, Mundo knows which travelers to avoid.

Pulling the leash or being wheeled in his crate, Mundo was our lead travel dog. Wherever we went, Mundo served as a filter, ever on the lookout for travelers sporting negative energy karmas. He was especially useful with humorless airport officials — ticket agents, customs men, federal security officers. Mundo served as the refractometer to a gemstone, a truth ray we could shine through people to reveal the true nature of their souls. Like a bank teller passing a hundred-dollar bill underneath the black light, we could immediately separate the good from the bad. Like at Kennedy Airport.

I.

"Well, where the hell is he?" demanded a crew cut with a coarse outer-borough accent. This was a newly-made-federal, white-shirt-with-three-American-flags-on-it, elite Homeland Security security guard.

"Where is who?"

"Your dog?"

"Where do you think he is?"

"Don't get smart with me."

"I'm only pointing out that your extra-large sign says he has to be in his crate, and so that might be the logical place to find him."

"Well, I can't search him in the crate."

"You're going to search him?"

"I need to frisk him."

So out wobbled Mundo, on unsure footing because of the sedatives Dr. Jimmy Jack, our vet, had prescribed. Mundo looked around confused, his blue eyes big as shooting marbles, locking like tractor beams on travelers and pulling them in. *He's so beautiful*, I heard five times. *It's demon*, I heard three. (*Yes, it is Demon*, I always reply to kids. *He's on his way to star in a new movie*. I mean, why not give them a thrill? *I touched Demon*, they run away to tell mommy.)

"I don't need to frisk him," the security man said.

"You're going to chance it?" I asked. What if he has a pair of nail clippers up his ass? Perhaps the guard just wanted to see how the dog would behave. This was probably part of his extensive post 9-11 double secret orange alert government training. *Dogs are ideal vessels for smuggling sharp instruments*, his manual reads. *Frisking all dogs is not feasible, but all should be put in the position to believe they will be frisked. Those who behave oddly may be then restrained and probed.*

 Mundo got back in his crate, and another white shirted man appeared. This man escorted us behind a cordon, into an elevator, and deep into Kennedy's underground labyrinth.

"Are we getting this treatment because he's royalty?" I asked.

"Everybody gets this ride," he said curtly, pressing a button to close the elevator door. He hadn't bothered to read Mundo's sign. "People worry about their pets," he said, sounding like it had been a real bother to get up and come to work. "They want to think they're in good hands."

"But they're really not?" Sometimes I can't resist. Especially with airline workers — anyone with a government-subsidized flashlight strapped to his belt — who act like they're doing travelers a real favor by showing up and earning forty dollars an hour. White shirt shrugged and turned away.

"This is where you say goodbye," white shirt said. "Say goodbye to Champ."

"His name's Mundo," I said. "It's written on the crate."

"Come on, Champ," he said. "Off we go."

I tried not to think about what would happen to Mundo next. I envisioned a half dozen bitter TSA white shirts shining their Mag-lites in his eyes and ramming sharpened broomsticks through his cage door, Mundo retreating and curling up in a corner, not even trying to defend himself.

II.

We finally made it out of the country. After changing planes in Helsinki, I looked out the window to see Mundo's crate coming up the conveyer belt to the baggage compartment. Hanging on to the crate, hunkered down to avoid banging his head on the fuselage doorway, a baggage handler was riding the belt with Mundo. I couldn't hear through the Plexiglas window, but I could see the man's lips moving. His face was two inches from the crate door, and he was talking to Mundo. I'm certain he was welcoming him aboard, reassuring him. As the crate neared the baggage hold, the conveyer belt stopped. The man eased Mundo's crate gently into the compartment and saluted him a *bon voyage*. Things were finally looking up.

From a bluebird sky we landed in Tallinn, took a long walk with Mundo, and a week later found ourselves in the island paradise of Ruhnu, visiting Liina's father. We had a wonderful time, romping through fairytale forests and swimming in the warm sea. But all that was to change.

After five days on the island, we missed our ferryboat to the mainland. Ferryboats come twice a week; it's not a boat you want to miss.

I blamed my wife, Liina, of course. We'd been sidetracked by her wanting to see two-dozen attractions on the way to the harbor. There was the couple with the summer kitchen done entirely in native stone. There was the man with a fish smoker made from a hollowed out oak tree. There were the 7,200 year-old seal hunting artifacts in the Ruhnu museum, which seemed to be closed except on days when the ferry ran. It was also blueberry season, and the forests were full of them.

Mundo, of course, enjoyed our hurried excursions. He urinated on the fish smoker and ate his fair share of blueberries, ripping them indelicately from bushes and chomping down until the white fur under his snout made it appear he'd devoured a small islander.

Liina chided me for being anal. "Relax, this isn't the German army," she said. "It's island time." Of course, when we reached the harbor, there was no ferryboat to be found. I'm sure I had that I-told-you-so grin all over my face, even though it did nothing for our relationship nor put us any closer to the mainland.

The harbormaster was out on the pier coiling rope and reported — with no hint of surprise in his voice — that the speck on the horizon was the ferryboat and that it had indeed left on time. It appeared we were going to spend another four days on the island, plenty of time to investigate the intricacies of fish smoker construction.

There was only one boat in the harbor, a 100-foot cruiser right off the set of Miami Vice, a Drug Lord Special with teak decks and a pair of jet-skis lashed on the stern. A fit, perfectly tanned couple was loading bicycles into the hold.

"Maybe they'll take us," Liina said. And maybe Malcolm Forbes would dock in his *Capitalist Tool* and have his helicopter pilot whisk us to the mainland.

The woman disappeared into the hold with a bicycle, and Arvo, Liina's father, wasted no time interrogating the man. Wouldn't the man like to take us to the mainland? Liina and I sat along the pier trying to look harmless and helpless, Norman Rockwell subjects suddenly adrift in Picasso's *Guernica*.

No, the man said, the dog might pee on the leather. Everything that wasn't teak was leather. And besides, he was going to Saaremaa.

Good enough, said Arvo. From Saaremaa ferries ran almost hourly to the mainland.

There was still the problem with the dog, noted the man.

"The dog," announced Arvo in his military, take-me-seriously-or-suffer-the-consequences voice, "is Mundo. And Mundo doesn't pee on anything he's not commanded to pee on."

The man was unimpressed. He stood on the pier in a pair of blue swim trunks with his arms crossed, smiling at Arvo. He didn't hate dogs, he explained, he just loved leather more.

Arvo motioned for his friend Tõnu to join him. Tõnu is a good six-four with a frame to carry it. The two men closed in around the svelte young speedboat captain.

"Listen," appealed Arvo. "I'm a diver."

"He's a diver," said Tõnu, taking another step forward, putting the young man in his shadow.

"With a boat like this, you may just need a diver someday," Arvo said. "You have hull problems, you're going to need a diver."

"You could use a diver," said Tõnu.

"And divers are expensive," added Arvo.

"Certainly can be," said Tõnu.

"I can get the job done for nothing," said Arvo.

"That's a good offer," said Tõnu.

"Tõnu, give me a pencil and paper." Arvo wrote his contact information down and handed it to the man.

"Still," the man said. "The dog."

By this time, the woman had emerged from the hold and was listening in.

"It's Mundo," said Arvo. "He's a prince."

"Oh, he's lovely," the woman shouted, seeing Mundo strike a man's-best-friend pose. When Mundo wants, he can exude all the cuddly qualities of a panda bear. The woman wore a lime-green bikini. Her muscles rippled as she jumped the gunwale onto the pier.

"Bring Mundo over here," shouted Arvo, and we abandoned our Rockwell poses to resemble a family of refugees fleeing the Nazis.

In seconds we had boarded the boat.

"I hope I need a diver soon," said the man, "before you forget your offer."

"I never forget," said Arvo, casting off lines. "You have a problem, call me."

Mundo curled up under a table on the deck out of the sun. The woman introduced herself as Jane and her boyfriend as Jaanus. Jaanus nosed the boat out to sea while Jane sat down with Mundo, him rolling over to allow her to scratch his belly.

"He's lovely," Jane said for the second or third time. She made no mention of Snow-dogs, and so we liked her all the more.

Jaanus set the autopilot to cruise toward Saaremaa at 25 knots, although 40 knots was the top speed. He was still breaking in the motor he said. Even at slightly over half-speed, we made the trip in exactly forty-five minutes. It had taken the ferryboat five hours to cover the same distance. Mundo spent the trip on deck in regal repose watching the girls take sun. I sat watching Jaanus, and wondered how someone so young and good-looking could become so fabulously wealthy without being a Hollywood actor or a Columbian drug lord.

When we docked in Saaremaa, we offered to take Jaanus and Jane to dinner. We were terribly grateful and wanted to show it through a gesture more significant than Mundo not staining the teak.

"We don't know much about Saaremaa restaurants," I offered, "but, really, anywhere you want to go. As long as the dog is welcome."

III.

"Dogs smell," declared an Estonian man who had thrown himself into a mass protest against Mundo boarding the microbus which would carry us across Saaremaa, board a ferry, and then travel two hours south to drop us in the mainland city of Pärnu. The protest group was led by a plump, ruddy woman carrying a pair of white plastic shopping bags. She had a look on her face like she'd just had something bad to eat.

"That dog does not come on this bus," she declared, pointing her crone finger at Mundo who was standing ready to find a seat, snout resting on the running board, eyes upward, locked on Liina, waiting for the command to board.

"The law says that if he's wearing a muzzle, he's welcome on public transportation," said Liina. "It's the law." The truth is she didn't know what the law said. We'd searched — we would have liked nothing better than to produce a copy of the law and wave it in a bus driver's face — and concluded that Estonia had no such law. In countries of the European Union, which Estonia had professed to join, a dog with a muzzle is legally welcome on buses. But Estonia has a ways to come before earning its EU membership. Only a few years earlier, Estonian bus drivers refused to allow seeing-eye dogs on buses, touching off a public incident which made international press. They came off as stereotypical backward Eastern Europeans, the kind who rarely bathe and will eagerly trade an Icarus bus for an old pair of Levi's.

"This isn't public transportation," the driver announced, siding with the plump woman and her male supporter. A few of the other passengers nodded, the driver's public declaration making it known which side they should support. Estonians are known for being very progressive — measured by mobile phone proliferation and liberal economic policy — but not all bus riders are. We had found a bus full of angry little people, anxious to strike a blow against perfumed foreigners and their purebred dogs. *Väikekodanlased* they're called. Bourgeoisie.

"Dogs smell," repeated the male passenger.

This struck me as ironic. If anyone smelled on the bus, it would likely be him. He was in his late forties, had uncombed hair, wore a forest green polyester jumpsuit and gray plastic shoes. I find many older Estonian men to be dapper gentlemen, men who are concerned with their appearance, who aren't afraid to wear a beret, men whose reflex is to rise in the presence of a lady. Young men are basically western, sometimes too much so, having taken MTV and Hollywood too literally, mimicking American action heroes in their dress and speech. But this man was stuck in the middle of those, part of the passed-by generation. Too old to adapt to the new ways, too young to retire.

"The law says …" Liina began.

"Maybe you can take him on a bigger bus, but he's not welcome here," ruled the driver. "This is a private company."

There was little sense arguing with these people. To them, this wasn't about a dog getting a ride on a bus. This was the French Revolution.

"Yeah!" shouted the woman with the shopping bags.

"Dogs smell," repeated the man, stomping a gray plastic shoe.

The other passengers nodded. Liina cried. Mundo looked around.

I went to get the ticket agent.

"The law says …" I took up where Liina left off.

"You should have told me you had a dog when you bought the tickets," said the agent.

"We did," I said. "My wife did."

"No, she didn't."

"Well, the law says …"

"The driver says no. You can take the dog on a bigger bus."

Liina was sitting on a bench in the shade sobbing. Passengers milled around ignoring her. Not a single one bothered to ask her if she was all right. Although this could happen anywhere, it is times like these when I have no affection for this country. I should have bought a car for the summer, I thought. Like Sherman McCoy said, one must insulate. Avoid the raggedy-assed multitudes. What harm can one dog do?

A big bus wasn't leaving for another six hours, so we exchanged our tickets and walked around, Mundo completely oblivious to our tragedy. That's what I respect about Mundo. He can forgive and forget. He's every bit as advanced as Tibetan lamas who say that every negative emotion — disappointment, unhappiness, anger — exists only in our mind. We manufacture them, and we can choose to dismiss them. Mundo only entertained the idea of disappointment for a moment — when he withdrew his head from the running board and looked back quizzically — but he never pouted. He moved on. He knew a fresh and better adventure was just around the corner. We don't need to go to Tibet. We have teachers in our midst.

We wandered back into town and sat down for breakfast at the nicest outdoor café we could find.

The waitress leaned down and scratched Mundo's ears. "He's so pretty," she said, as he rolled on his back and put his feet in the air. "May I give him some scraps from the kitchen?"

IV.

Several weeks later, Lilli, Liina's sister, offered us a ride to the island of Hiiumaa. We couldn't say no. After traveling by bus, always on guard for *väikekodanlased* — or the unenlightened as Mundo might refer to them — to protest Mundo's presence, the privacy of a car was a real treat.

Lilli, if she ever reads this, will take offence at my description of her, but I'm just stating the facts: Lilli is a soccer mom. She has two kids, one dog, and a minivan. I love her minivan. There's plenty of room for Mundo and all of my fishing gear, and Lilli is such a clean freak that the van is always put back in pristine condition even before I've thought to show my gratitude by vacuuming Mundo's hair. That van is, well, sanitary. But she's not like American soccer moms. She's not worried about bacteria. She doesn't carry a box of those handiwipes everywhere insisting her kids clean their hands after touching a handrail or a doorknob. But cleanliness is something in Lilli's genetic code. She has to clean everything. So no more dirty bus floors for Mundo. We were going to Hiiumaa in a clean car.

Mundo is always offered the rear seat, and sometimes he obliges, riding back there until a conversation or an argument starts, something he's not yet a part of. Then he bounds over two rows of seats to sit on the floor near the stick shift. In the middle of things he sleeps well.

He sleeps soundly until we arrive in the ferryboat queue where he knows it's his job to help buy a ticket. Then he's let off leash to swim in a rocky area near the port. When it's warm enough, we swim with him until it's time to board and then we run for the ramp, racing ahead of the cars so we can get a good place to sit.

Dogs are welcome on ferryboats, more or less, and so I was surprised when a uniformed steward approached me. "Dogs," she said, "must be outside."

"I'm just passing through," I said, indicating the doorway to the aft deck. I didn't know how to get him aft without passing through the restaurant. There was a miniature schnauzer curled up under a restaurant table, barking at us as we passed, his owners sitting quietly enjoying a cup of tea. Of course this begs the question — but sometimes it's best just not to ask. We kept walking.

The Hiiumaa ferries aren't the nicest boats around, but they're pretty good, considering their only function is to transport people from the mainland to an island inhabited by two thousand people. The ferry company bought the old Soviet ferries that ran the Tallinn-Helsinki route, those far too small to handle current passenger traffic. You can't connect two northern European countries with any kind of transportation and not have a bar, and this ferry has a large one. It's a carpeted room that faces aft and is staffed by a nice pair of middle-aged ladies who probably do most of their travel, when not on the ferry, by bus. There's a large sign on the glass door to the bar, a white silhouette of a dog with a red circle around and slash through the animal. But the dog depicted in that sign is a shorthaired breed, and it's because of this, I suppose, that the two nice ladies have always welcomed Mundo in the bar.

The bar is connected to the kitchen, and so I always order a schnitzel to go with my large Albert le Coq beer. I'm not sure what schnitzel is, but it resembles a chicken fried steak and is occasionally stuffed with cheese. It's cheap, filling, and Mundo likes it, too.

At this point, I would like to qualify that Mundo never begs. It could be because Liina strictly forbids me feeding him from the table. But I like to think that he's naturally dignified, that he wouldn't take it, even if offered. He would wait for me to carry it out on deck, where there would be no chance of staining the carpet.

"Give him that piece," says Liina.

I'm surprised by her change of heart. It never bothered me to feed him from the table. I had always done it when she wasn't looking. I reach for the chunk of meat. It's gray with breadcrumbs fried around it.

"No," she says. "Not that way." She reaches across the table, lifts my plate, and puts it on the floor under the table. Mundo goes to work, delicately lifting the piece of schnitzel off the plate before lying down to eat it. Heads turn. I'm thinking my fellow passengers may object to a dog licking a plate they may receive on the return trip, but most are smiling.

Mundo finishes the schnitzel, my potatoes too. He returns to his seated, ready position.

"May I?" I hear the man next to me ask. I turn to see that he too has a plate full of leftovers.

Why not, I shrug, and Mundo is presented another meal. This time it's *pihvid*, a variation on a theme of beef. It looks just like the schnitzel, not that it matters to Mundo.

On the other side of the man sits a woman eating pancakes with mushroom filling. "Ask first," she tells her son, sliding the plate across the table to him.

"Go ahead," I say, and Mundo is deep in his third repast.

Somehow, the *pihvid* and the pancakes touch off a chain reaction. Random people rise one by one to bring Mundo their plates. First it's mostly children, afraid of nothing and interested to make Mundo's acquaintance. Each waits patiently for Mundo to do his work and then removes the clean plate and returns to his seat. Then a few adults start to come. An old woman gathers the scraps from her table and presents her plate to Mundo.

This seems almost organized, perhaps pre-ordained. That Mundo, Crown Prince of Estonia, Governor of Kõpu Peninsula, Rightful Heir to All Surveyed, has finally come home, finally honored by his subjects in a fashion befitting his station. I look to the bar to see that everyone in line has turned to watch His Majesty eat. The two middle-aged bar maids have stopped serving and stand with curious grins. They are perhaps upset about the plates. More likely, they are wondering if Mundo would like a beer with that.

Acknowledgements

Back in Estonia, thanks to editors Barbi Pilvre, Priit Hõbemägi, Sigrid Kõiv, and Neeme Korv for finding room for my work in their pages. Thanks to translators Erkki Sivonen and Marek Laane, who keep my Estonian-language columns respectable. The Diel brothers (Scott in Estonia, Stan in the US) were kind to contribute their help editing the collection. My brother Villu ("Viltu" to family) for his behind-the-scenes work. Guillaume (now in Portland) for getting me out of the house.

Special thanks to Liina, who has patiently suffered through being the subject of many columns. She is the love of my life and possibly the world's best sport.